Walkers', Cyclists' and Horse Riders'

Lightfoot Guide
to the
The Three Saints' Way
Winchester to Mont St Michel
Along the Millenium Footpath Trail and the Chemin Anglais

243 Kilometres

Copyright © 2008 Pilgrimage Publications All rights reserved.
ISBN: 978-2-917183-04-5

Also by Babette Gallard and Paul Chinn
Riding the Milky Way 2006
Riding the Roman Way 2007
LightFoot Guides to the via Francigena 2008
Reflections - A Pictorial Journey Along the via Francigena 2008
LightFoot Guide to the Plantagenet Way - Mont St Michel to St Jean d'Angely 2008
Reflections - A Pictorial Journey Along theThree Saint's Way 2008

The authors have done their best to ensure the accuracy and currency of the information in the LightFoot Guide to the Chemin Anglais, however, they can accept no responsibility for any loss, injury or inconvenience sustained by any traveller as a result of information contained in the guide. Changes will inevitably occur within the lifespan of this edition and the authors welcome notification of such changes and any other feedback that will enable them to enhance the quality of the guide.

Pilgrimage Publications is a not-for-profit organisation dedicated to the identification and mapping of pilgrim routes all over the world, regardless of religion or belief. Any revenue derived from the sale of guides or related activities is used further to enhance the service and support provided to pilgrims.

Pilgrimage Publications has been created by Paul Chinn and Babette Gallard, two people who have covered many hundreds of pilgrim kilometres. The ethos of their operation is based on four 4 key aims:
1. To enable walkers, cyclists and riders to follow pilgrim routes all over the world.
2. To ensure Pilgrimage Publications guides are as current as possible, using pilgrim feedback as a major source of information.
3. To produce LightFoot Guides or any other materials using only the most environmentally friendly option currently available.
4. To promote eco-friendly travel.

Tracing Yesterday Using Today's Technology

LightFoot Guides are designed to enable everyone to meet his/her personal goals and enjoy the best, whilst avoiding the worst, of following ancient pilgrimage routes. Written for Walkers, Cyclists and Horse Riders, every section of the LightFoot guide to the Chemin Anglais provides specific information for each group.

LightFoot Guides provide metre-by-metre instructions based on GPS co-ordinates, supported by Online Updates and are produced using the Print On Demand method - the most environmentally friendly option currently available.

The authors would also like to emphasise that they have made great efforts to use only public footpaths and to respect private property. Historically, pilgrims may not have been so severely restricted by ownership rights and the pressures of expanding populations, but unfortunately this is no longer the case. Today, even the most free-spirited traveller must adhere to commonly accepted routes. Failure to do so will only antagonise local residents, encourage the closure of routes - some examples of which have already been encountered - and selfishly detract from the experience of the pilgrims following on behind.

Revised editions of this guide will be published each year, but everyone is advised to refer to the relevant update page on the Pilgrimage Publications website, because changes will be immediately listed here when they are received.

ACKNOWLEDGEMENTS
Pilgrimage Publications has been developed and supported by more people than could possibly be listed here, but the authors would particulary like to thank the following individuals for their contribution to this first LightFoot Guide to the via Francignea:
Barbara Edgar, for her thorough, sometimes painful (for the authors) proof-reading.
Marion Marples, Confraternity of St James, for her expert input and for highlighting the need for this guide.
Jeffrey Salter, for his stunningand highly professional photographs of Mont St Michel.

Please complete and return this form in order to:
* Suggest changes
* Receive GPS route data
* Receive regular email guide updates
* Receive information on latest and future publications

Alternatively, complete the online form: www.pilgrimagepublications.com

Name:	
Address:	
email:	
website:	
Date Guide Book Purchased:	
Where Guide Book Purchased	
Items for Change/Notification	

Please send your completed form to: Pilgrimage Publications, 40, rue de la Pinterie, 35300 FOUGÈRES, FRANCE

CONTENTS	PAGE
About Pilgrimages and Pilgrims	5
About the Three Saints' Way	6
About Your LightFoot Guide to the Chemin Anglais	7
About Maps and Map Symbols	8
About Signs Along the Route and the Pilgrim Record	9
About Travel	10
About the Basics in Britain	13
About the Basics in France	14
About Transporting Horses	15
About Transporting Dogs	16
About Useful Links and Reading	17
About General French Vocabulary	18
About Cycling/Equine French Vocabulary	19
Winchester to Bishops Waltham	21
Bishops Waltham to Portsmouth	30
Portsmouth to Barfleur	36
Barfleur to Saint-Vaast-le-Hougue	40
Saint-Vaast-la-Hougue to le Bourg de Lestre	44
le Bourg de Lestre to Montebourg	48
Montebourg to Sainte-Mère-Eglise	52
Sainte-Mère-Eglise to Sainte-Marie-du-Mont	56
Sainte-Marie-du-Mont to Carentan	59
Carentan to Saintenay	63
Saintenay to Périers	66
Périers to Saint-Sauveur-Landelin	70
Saint-Sauveur-Landelin to Coutances	72
Coutances to Regnéville-sur-Mer	76
Regnéville sur Mer to les Salines	80
les Salines to Granville	86
Granville to Carolles Plage	92
Carolles-Plage to Genêts	98
Genêts to le Mont Saint Michel	102
Map Reference Chart	107
Pilgrim Record	109

The idea of sacred motion or travel runs deep in human religion, dating back to when early humans would climb hilltops to be closer to God or go to a specific spot to dance around in circles.

Spiritual talk is full of the language of travel : walking the walk, leaving behind, stepping forward and following God's paths on our spiritual journey of life.

Christian pilgrims have travelled across Europe since medieval times and for a variety of reasons. The majority would have been heading for three main sites of devotion, mostly on foot, covering anything up to 20 or 30 kilometres a day and usually carrying one of the three pilgrimage emblems: a scallop shell for Santiago de Compostela in Spain, keys for Saint Peter in Rome and a cross or palm leaf for Jerusalem. For some the motivation would have been entirely religious, but for many others it was far more basic and earthly - the sick hoping saintly relics would cure their bodily ills, criminals forced to take the long haul as a custodial sentence and the rest banking on enhanced pilgrim credibility and status when they got back home.

Today's Pilgrim

"To set out on a pilgrimage is to throw down a challenge to everyday life."
Phil Cousineau - the Art of Pilgrimage

The pilgrimage is experiencing a renaissance. In 1986, just 2,491 pilgrims collected their Compostela certificate in Santiago, but by 2006 these figures had passed the 100,000 mark. Today's pilgrimage attracts people of all ages and beliefs, their primary common factor being the need to stand back from the daily pressures and take time to reflect on their lives and the lives of those around them. Most pilgrims choose to travel on foot, but others opt for bicycles, horses, cars or even public transport.

Today's pilgrims also travel for a variety of reasons other than the strictly devout, but ultimately, whatever the original motivation, everyone will find themselves changed by the experience, including the people living along the route who will profit from a cross-cultural exchange and of course the pilgrim trade. Travelling as a Pilgrim can only ever be at the speed your own body and mental attitude will allow, which may initially seem like a restriction. However, even the most cynical and reluctant newcomer will quickly realize that this is in fact a first step on the road to freedom. Clearly there will be days when you wonder why the hell you are there, but rest assured, this is only a temporary condition and you will find the answer in the people you meet and the memories you take away.

Road to the Stars

From the 9th century, pilgrims have followed the route of the sun to the west and at night they replaced this with a stream of stars, the Milky Way. The aim of their journey was to visit the tomb of St. James the Great, one of the twelve apostles of Christ, who tradition believes to be entombed in the cathedral of Santiago de Compostela. Many of those early pilgrims would have been making their way to the four main starting points of the St James Way in France, which suggests that today there should be clearly identifiable routes. Of course the reality is that they chose a variety of roads, paths and sometimes open country to suit their personal requirements, and it is only in today's organized and prescribed environment that we look for the single Pilgrim route. The name, Three Saint's Way, has been created by the authors of your LightFoot guide and is based on the three saints associated with this pilgrimage: St Swithin, St Michael and St James. Far from being a single route, it is in fact a collection of intersecting routes, comprised of the Millenium Footpath Trail in England and the *Chemin Anglais* in France, which ultimately leads onto the Way of St James in St Jean d'Angely. This guide covers the first section of the route, starting in Winchester, England, and then continuing in France from Barfleur to Mont St Michel. The second, *Chemin Anglais*, takes pilgrims to St Jean d'Angely where the route intersects with the Way of St James starting from Paris.

Saint Swithin was famous for charitable gifts and building churches. Only one miracle is attributed to Swithin while he was alive. An old lady's eggs had been smashed by workmen building a church. Swithin picked the broken eggs up and, it is said, they miraculously became whole again. Swithin died on 2 July 862. His grave just outside the west door of the Old Minster, so that people would walk across it and rain fall on it, in accordance with Swithin's wishes. On 15 July 971, Swithin's remains were dug up and moved to a shrine in the cathedral by Bishop Ethelwold. Miraculous cures were associated with the event, and Swithin's feast day is the date of the removal of his remains, not his death day. However, the removal was also accompanied by ferocious and violent rain storms that lasted 40 days and 40 nights and are said to indicate the saint's displeasure at being moved. This is probably the origin of the legend that if it rains on Saint Swithin's feast day, the rain will continue for 40 more days. Saint Swithin is also the patron of Winchester Cathedral.

The Cult of St Michael - Churches dedicated to St Michael are often built on the top of hills or mountains. St Michael is said to have appeared to the Bishop of Avranches, St Aubert, in 708 and instructed him to build a church on the rocky mound. When the Bishop repeatedly delayed, St Michael is said to have burned a hole in the Bishop's skull with his finger. Michael is usually depicted as an angel, standing over a dragon, sometimes piercing it. [He is also shown as the angel of judgment, holding scales and balancing the souls of the good and evil.] In 1467 the Order of St Michael was established in France. Members of the Order wore a gold collar with a medallion of St Michael fighting the serpent standing on Mont-Saint-Michel. The gold chain was made of scallop shells, the symbol of pilgrimage in general and to Santiago in particular. There was an early monastic foundation from the 7th century and in the 11th century a new church was built.

Using Your Lightfoot Guide
This book traces the Chemin Anglais from Winchester to Mont St Michel. In it you will find an introductory section followed by 19 chapters, each of which covers a segment of the route.
Each chapter contains:
*A route summary
*A cultural and historical overview of the region
*Detailed Instructions
*Map

Accommodation Listings:
Accommodation prices are based on one double room per night - accurate at the time of entry, but subject to change. For simplicity, the listing is divided into 3 price bands:

B1 0-20 €/£   B2 21-50 €/£   B3 51-70 €/£

In general there are no listings above 60€ per night, unless nothing else is available in the area. Prices may or may not include breakfast and some establishments charge a tariff for dogs.

Layout
The entire distance has been divided into manageable sections of approximately 15 kilometres, but accommodation (where it exists) is listed for the entire length of the section so that is up to you and your body where you decide to stop.

Instructions
The entire route has been GPS traced (a total of 1300 waypoints and routing instructions) and logged using way point co-ordinates. On this basis, it should be possible to navigate the route using only the written instructions, though a map is provided for additional support and general orientation. Use of a compass is recommended.

Each instruction sheet provides:
*Detailed directions corresponding to GPS way point numbers on the map
*Verification Point - additional verification of current position
*Distance (in metres) between each way point

Each map provides:
*A north/south visual representation of the route with way point numbers
*Icons indicating places to stay, monuments etc. (see Map symbols)
*Relevant signs to look out for along the route
*Map reference number/s for the section

About Maps and Map Symbols

✕	Restaurant
☕	Café
⌐	Accommodation
🛒	Grocery
⋀	Campsite
𝒊	Tourist Information Office
🚂	Railway Station
🐴	Equestrian Centre
♜	Monument
✈	Airfield
⛪	Major church or other religious building
♀	Parish church
──┼──	Canal
──┼──	Railway
────	River
▮▮▮	Motorway or major road
▮▮▮	Main road
═══	Minor road
━ ━	Chemin Anglais on road
▪ ▪ ▪	Chemin Anglais off road
━ ━	Alternate route - on road
▪ ▪ ▪	Alternate route - off road

8

Urban waymarking

Countryside waymarking

In Hampshire, England, the trail's Waymarks are based on the green silhouette of Mont St Michel and include the shell and pilgrim staff long associated with pilgrimages to Santiago de Compostela.

Signs to Look Out For:
In France the paths you will be following are signposted by: the FFRP (Federation Française de la Randonnée Pédestre), the Friends of Chemin de Mont St Michel and the Friends of the Chemin de St Jacques.

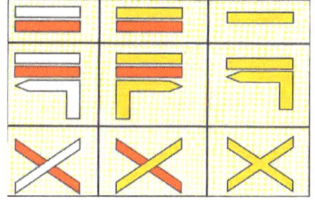

Pilgrim Record

A pilgrim's record was and still is used as proof of pilgrim status and to provide a pilgrimage log. Hampshire County Council (Hampshire County Council Information Centre, Mottisfont Court, High Street, Winchester SO23 8ZB. Tel: 0044 (0)345 626424/870500 expuwin@hants.gov.uk) can provide a small Pilgrim Record for the English section, but for a longer one designed to accommodate more stamps, you can either use the one provided at the end of this guide book or contact the Confraternity of St James (see useful links).

In England your pilgrim record can be stamped at the following four locations in Hampshire:

Winchester Cathedral - please ask at the cathedral's entrance for directions.
Tel: 0044 (0)1962 857227
Open all year: 09.00 to 17.00 daily

Bishops Waltham's Palace - main ticket office.
Tel: 0044 (0)1489 892460
Open   01 April to 30 September: 10.00 to 18.00
            01 to 31 October: 10.00 to 17.00
Closed   01 November to 31 March
Special 15% discount on normal admission prices for Pilgrim Trail Record Holders.

Portsmouth
Port Manager's Enquiry Office at their ferry terminal.
Information Desk on board any P&O Portsmouth to Cherbourg.
Tel: 0044 (0)870 2424 999

In France, most hotels, tourist offices and of course churches will provide stamps for your pilgrim record.

Food, drink and a place to collapse at the end of the day

This route attracts only a fraction of the number of pilgrims found on the Way of St James from Paris and has the corresponding number of pilgrim hostels - very few. Similarly, do not expect to meet cohorts of pilgrims, this is an undeveloped route, which brings its own advantages, but it is an aspect everyone needs to be aware of before starting out. The **English section** - Winchester to Portsmouth (also known as the Millenium Footpath Trail) - is relatively short and through a well populated area, meaning you are unlikely to die of hunger or thirst on the way, though if you are looking for accommodation to break the section, then you are advised to book ahead. **The French section** is better than some areas in central France, but be aware that France has sold its soul to the car and hyper market, with the result that you will be lucky to find a café or shop in anything smaller than a town. And even if you do, you can bet your bottom Euro that it will be closed for lunch or *en vacances*. In short, the watch-word is assume the worst, carry food for the day, stop where you know you can replenish your supplies and always phone ahead to ensure that the place you have chosen to stay in still exists, is open and has a room available for the night you need it. But, having given you a bleak view of France, it is also important to stress that the French are extremely welcoming and a knock on the door of the local priest or *Mairie* will usually end in a solution.

Cyclists - To Road or Off-road

Quite simply if you are a Road Biker our route is not for you, though of course it is possible

to follow an approximate version of the *Chemin Anglais* by using road maps. Off-road bikers can go just about anywhere a walker or horse can, but there are occasions when the pain/pleasure ratio makes other options preferable and sensible. We have ridden both horses and bikes the length of the route and know the disadvantages and pleasures of each, so it is with this experience in mind that we offer alternatives where we think it necessary. Of course ultimately these are only guidelines and everyone has to make their own choice. In terms of what kind of bikes you should use, clearly something fairly robust.

Horses and Riders - to Go or not to Go

Make no mistake, riding along the *Chemin Anglais* is going to be full of unexpected

challenges. For people travelling without back-up, finding fodder and a place to stay will be the greatest challenge, but turning up in a village or town with a horse and a Don Quixote air can have the most amazing, invariably positive, outcomes. The route itself is possibly the easiest and most enjoyable long distance ride the authors have experienced to date. A great deal is off-road, through stunning countryside and with no real challenges. There are a number of equestrian establishments listed along the way, but essentially pilgrim riders must use their initiative and be prepared to ask for help. As for farriers and vets, they are also listed, but of course we cannot guarantee their competence or availability.

Signs Are Not Always What They Seem To Be

It is a feature of French roads that the responsibility for their maintenance can be transferred between state and commune. The most obvious change is in the number, which can be confusing for the uninitiated. Basically it is very simple. *Route Nationale* or 'N' roads can become minor roads, classed as 'D' roads, which means dropping the N, adding a D and then a number - for example the N32 is now the D1032.

Behaviour on the Road - preserve our heritage

Following pilgrim routes on foot, bicycle or horse is potentially the most eco-friendly form of travel possible. It can also benefit the local economy so that pilgrim tourists are always welcome, but this will only be the case if a few very simple rules are followed. Some sections of popular pilgrim routes are ruined by pilgrim detritus: plastic bottles, bags, tissues, sanitary towels, toilet paper ... an unsightly mess that is also a great deal more serious for the environment and wildlife. Everyone is responsible for the maintenance of these historic routes and should dispose of their rubbish in the appropriate way. Horse riders face an additional responsibility in this respect, because horses/donkeys can destroy turf and decimate gardens in seconds. Large piles of steaming, fly-clustered manure outside a restaurant are not good for trade and people do not like having metal shod hooves on their open-toed sandals. Whether you are walking, cycling or riding, please think about these points when you are travelling

Health and Safety

The most general and obvious health and safety tips apply to everyone; walker, cyclist or rider. This route should present no serious problems even to a beginner, provided you follow a few simple rules.

✴ Don't take unnecessary risks by tackling overly long or difficult routes.
✴ Know where you are or have a map and the ability to read it.
✴ On longer walks, be aware of "escape routes" in case you need to cut your walk short.
✴ Make sure you have plenty to eat and drink and are adequately dressed for the length of time you'll be out.
✴ Check the forecast before you set out and keep an eye on the sky. Rain, mist or fog and cold are the obvious hazards.
✴ The route recommended by this guide avoids roads wherever possible, but you will encounter some. In these situations, use the pavement if there is one and safe crossings wherever possible.

Walkers

Walking up hills increases the work load and energy cost considerably; even walking down again uses more energy than walking on the flat. Walking downhill can also make you sore if you're unaccustomed to it, because it uses muscles as shock absorbers. Plan rest days to allow your muscles and feet to recover. There is some controversy over how to treat blisters when they do occur. Some walkers prefer to burst the blister carefully and immediately apply a sterile dressing. Others argue this runs the risk of infection, and instead recommend gel-filled blister plasters. Either way, injuries and blisters are miserable and if serious enough can put an end to your plan, so avoidance is the best tactic.

Rucksack: the general principle should be to carry only what you need and no more. This route will not take you far away from civilization and on most days shops, hotels and hostels will be easily accessible, though riders with horses may have to plan further ahead. In all cases your rucksack should be large enough to take a tent and sleeping bag, if only as a fallback measure if things go awry.

Footwear: You will only need a pair of light walking boots, because you will not encounter any severe climbs (in France at least), but you should take a pair of comfortable sandals or trainers to give your feet a break at the end of the day.

Clothing: waterproofs are a must, along with a fleece for the cooler evenings. Plan according to the time of year that you are travelling, but never rely on the weather. It will always do the unexpected.

Cyclists

The reality of long distance unsupported cycling trips is that you have to carry everything with you, and you have to wash clothes every night so Lycra is a good option. If you are thinking of cycling, you probably have your own bicycle already and providing it is a reasonable quality mountain bike, it will be adequate. Try to minimise the weight you are carrying. The more weight the greater the energy output required to carry it. There is a wide variety of racks available to support your panniers, but choose one of solid construction because it will take a lot of punishment. The mountings and securing nuts must be checked daily.

Injuries: The most common causes of cycling-related injuries are incorrect riding posture, such as putting too much weight on the hands and riding with straight elbows. Knee injury is generally due to overuse and occurs when a cyclist is doing too much, too fast. Once you've crested the hill, avoid the temptation to coast down the other side. Pedal a little bit to reduce the risk of lactic acid build-up in your leg muscles.

Horses and Riders

Don't even consider going on the *Chemin Anglais* with your horse or donkey before you have ensured that:
* He/she is one hundred percent traffic proof
* He/she is familiar with crowds and generally noisy places
* He/she can be tethered for a full night
* He/she can deal with a variety of different feeds.

Equipment: The equipment you take will be governed by two factors: importance and weight - two priorities you must literally weigh up before leaving. There are probably as many opinions as riders on the best equipment to be used, so we will not enter that particular minefield here. Use the tack that you know your horse can tolerate for extended distances without suffering from galls and use a saddle pad that will distribute the weight as much as possible. Another point to note is that you will meet difficult terrain, so make sure all of your equipment will stay in place on both steep climbs and descents. Be sure to test it all before you leave. Despite all of your best endeavours your equipment will be lost, stolen or worn out by the time you return home, so be sure that what you take you will be happy to lose. If you want to use a pack pony, consult the professionals and make sure you test your gear and your pony thoroughly before you go. Don't carry a huge veterinary kit. A can of antiseptic spray, an anti-inflammatory gel or something similar, and (if you are allowed to) a course of antibiotics, is ample. You can find vets and chemists along the route without any difficulty.

Absolutely indispensable:
* Canvas water buckets
* Plastic gloves and plastic bags to pick up the inevitable equine accident. Horse riders have as much responsibility for the behaviour of their horses as do dog owners for their dogs.
* We recommend leather chaps, a waterproof cape and a broad brimmed hat.

So there you have it, the few words of wisdom we have to offer. Pilgrim feedback is fundamental for the accurate maintenance of the information in this guide, so please let us know where the route has changed, our information is incorrect or you can add to what we have. And remember, you are not doing this for us, but for all the pilgrims who will follow in your footsteps.

The British currency is the pound sterling. A few of the big shops will accept Euros, but it is rarely used in Britain. **Standard Banking Hours Monday-Friday 09:30 - 15.30.** Some branches stay open until 17.30, and a few are open Saturday morning. Most banks will have an ATM (Automated Teller Machine) outside the bank where you can draw out money with a credit or debit card. Many of these are available to use 24 hours a day, but some do still close for a few hours during the night.

Post Offices: Standard Opening Hours / 09.00 - 17.30 Monday - Friday. Few open on Saturday morning and are increasingly found as counters within other shops. Post Offices are shut on Sundays and Bank Holidays.

There are **public telephones** in many places. Some of them also give internet access. Illustrations and instructions demonstrate how to use the phone. Calls can be paid for with coins, a phonecard or a credit card. **Emergencies - 999 will give you access to the following services:** Fire, Police, Ambulance, Coastguard, Mountain rescue or Cave rescue. This is free and can be dialled from any telephone (including mobile phones) in the UK. (You can also dial 112 in the UK and any other European country).

Basic Business Hours
Mondays - Saturdays 09.00 - 17.30, though some shopping centres stay open until 8 pm or later. Sunday - 10.00 - 16.00, though Sunday shopping has become popular in recent years and most large shops in towns are open for business. Shops are only allowed to trade for 6 hours on Sundays. On public holidays some shops open and some shops do not. Nearly all shops are closed on Christmas and New Year Day. Most shopping centres are closed on Easter Sunday with reduced shopping hours on Easter Monday. In villages, some rural shops still follow the tradition of an early closing day (usually a Wednesday) when they close at 13.00pm.

All EU citizens are eligible for free health care if they have the correct documentation. Non EU Citizens must arrange personal health insurance.

British food has traditionally been based on beef, lamb, pork, chicken and fish and generally served with potatoes and one other vegetable, but now you can eat any meal from just about every culture - the Indian curry probably being the most popular. You will find that food is served at just about every hour of the day, but rarely cheaply.

English hotels are graded from zero to five stars and the price more or less corresponds to the number of stars. **Bed and Breakfast** (B&B). Guests have accommodation in private houses and are served breakfast by the owner, who often has useful local knowledge. **Youth Hostels** provide accommodation where guests can rent a bed (sometimes a bunk bed) in a dormitory and share a common bathroom, kitchen, and lounge. You will need to be a member of the International Youth Hostel Federation (www.ehic.org.uk)

As the birthplace of **camping**, England has a large number of places to stay of every kind – from small, quiet spots to big lively parks offering a wide range of facilities and entertainment. Camping and caravan parks are excellent for families - they offer great value for money in a friendly environment. They are located both near the coast and in the heart of the countryside.

Currency: Euro. Standard banking Hours: Monday-Friday 09.30-12.00 and 14.00-16.00. Closed on Sundays and usually Monday, with half day opening on Saturday morning

Post Offices (La Poste): Standard opening hours Mon - Fri - 09.30-12.00 and 14.00-17.00. Half day opening on Saturday morning.

You can make **domestic and international phone calls** from any **public telephone box** and can receive calls where there is a new logo of a ringing bell.

Emergencies - 112 will give you access to the following services: Fire, Police, Ambulance, Coastguard, Mountain rescue or Cave rescue. This is free and can be dialled from any telephone (including mobile phones).

Basic Business Hours - 08.00-12.00 and 14.00-18.00. Almost everything in France - shops, museums, tourist offices etc. - closes for two hours at midday. Food shops often don't reopen until half way through the afternoon, but close at 19.30 or 20.00. The standard closing days are Sunday and Monday in small towns, but you will find that many large supermarkets are now staying open throughout the day.

All EU citizens are eligible for free health care if they have the correct documentation.

In France, the best way to eat breakfast is in a bar or café, at a fraction of the cost charged by most hotels. Expect a croissant or some bread with coffee or hot chocolate. At lunchtime and sometimes in the evenings you'll find most cafés and restaurants offering a *plat du jour*, which is by far the cheapest alternative if you don't fancy cooking yourself.

Internet Cafés - France is generally well-served with internet cafés, though finding a reliable directory for a fully comprehensive list has not been easy. Nevertheless Most Tourist Offices will provide access at 0.50€ per 15 mins, as do the public libraries.

In country areas, in addition to standard hotels, you will come across **chambre d'hôtes** and **ferme auberge**, bed and breakfast accommodation in someone's house or farm. These are rarely an especially cheap option, usually costing the equivalent of a two star hotel.

Youth hostels (*auberges de jeunesse***)** are great for travellers on a budget. They are often beautifully sited and they allow you to cut costs by preparing your own food in their kitchens or eating in cheap canteens. The majority will require that you are a member of the International Youth Hostel Federation.

Gites d'étape are basic but do not require membership and provide bunk beds with primitive kitchen and washing facilities at a reasonable price.

Campsites in France are nearly always clean and have plenty of hot water. On the coast there are superior categories of campsite where you will pay prices similar to those of a hotel for the facilities -bars, restaurants and usually elaborate swimming pools too. For horses, it is useful to know that campsite owners often allow horses to be tethered at the edge of the site.

Horses

If you are starting out from the UK with your horse you will need the following:

1. Export licence
Licence required to take your horse or pony out of the UK. The ferry company will ask for this at the port when you arrive to board the ferry. You can apply for this yourself from DEFRA (Department for Environment, Food and Rural Affairs), include the proof of value for ponies.

2. TRACES document
You can apply to DEFRA yourself or get your vet to apply for the health certificate for the country your horse is travelling to. The certificate will be sent directly to your vet and you will need to make an appointment with him or her for the horse to be inspected no more than 48 hours before it leaves the UK. The ferry company will ask to see this at the port but will return it to you. You will need this in your destination country. You will need a health certificate to be issued and signed in your destination country to be able to return to the UK (not applicable for France or Ireland).

3. Route Plan
A form which you partially complete and then send off with your application for a health certificate. DEFRA will stamp the first section and send it back with the health certificate for you to complete during the journey. Do not allow any official to keep this en route. You must take this home and keep it for 6 months in case DEFRA want to inspect it.

For all initial export queries go to:
International Animal Health Division
Service Delivery Unit
Ceres House
2 Searby Road
Lincoln, LN2 4DT
Tel: 01522 563132
Fax: 01522 545014
Email: lincoln.iahsdu@animalhealth.gsi.gov.uk

For DEFRA: www.defra.gov.uk/

For more general information and assistance:
http://www.gettingoutofhere.co.uk/horses.html

Dogs Travelling under the Pet Travel Scheme (PETS) - eligible in all EU countries

Dogs can enter the UK under PETS as long as they meet the rules, but they must not have been outside any of the EU or non-EU listed countries in the 6 calendar months before travelling to the UK.
Dogs that are resident in either the United Kingdom or one of the other qualifying countries can enter or re-enter the UK without quarantine provided they meet the rules of the Scheme.

For list of countries go to:
www.defra.gov.uk/animalh/quarantine/pets/procedures/support-info/other.htm

Animals from unlisted countries must spend 6 months in quarantine on arrival in the UK. There are no requirements for pets travelling directly between the UK and the Republic of Ireland.
PETS procedures can be carried out in any of the listed qualified countries.

The six month rule for entry or re-entry to the UK
Your dog or cat may not enter the UK under PETS until six calendar months have passed from the date that your vet took the blood sample which led to a satisfactory test result (see below). Once the vet has issued the PETS documentation and that six month period has passed, the PETS documentation is valid for your pet to enter the UK.

The procedures:
* Before any of the other procedures for PETS are carried out, your pet must be fitted with a microchip so that it can be properly identified.
* Have your pet vaccinated.
* After the microchip has been fitted your pet must be vaccinated against rabies. There is no exemption to this requirement, even if your pet has a current rabies vaccination.
* Arrange a blood test
* After your pet has been vaccinated, it must be blood tested to make sure that the vaccine has given it a satisfactory level of protection against rabies.
* Get PETS documentation.

For animals being prepared in an EU country, you should get an EU pet passport. If you are preparing your animal in a non-EU listed country you will need to obtain an official third country veterinary certificate although note that Gibraltar, Norway, San Marino and Switzerland are also issuing passports. Before your pet re-enters the UK, it must be treated against ticks and a tapeworm not less than 24 hours and not more than 48 hours before it is checked in with an approved transport company for its journey into the UK.

Be warned - you must check with the ferry company whether you are allowed to take your dog outside a vehicle.

For More Information:
PETS Helpline on 0870 241 1710
www.defra.gov.uk/animalh/quarantine/pets/index.htm

www.PilgrimsTales.com	Pilgrim Tales, passionate about inspiring others with the possibility of discovery, understanding and peace through travel
www.theexpeditioner.com	The Expeditioner, travel-themed webzine.
www.csj.org.uk	Confraternity of st James providing a wealth of information about the many pilgrim routes to Santiago de Compostela in Spain as well as general guidance and advice to pilgrims.
www.stjamesirl.com	Irish Society of the Friends of St James The Irish equivalent of the CSJ.
www.scottishwalkingsticks.com/	A very brief example of how to make a stick by Derek Farrar.
www.thestickman.co.uk/	A commercial site by Keith Pickering but good for purchasing DIY stick-making supplies.
www.visitwinchester.co.uk/site/things-to-do/tours-and-trails/long-distance-walking-routes	Winchester City Council Site with references to Millenium Footpath Trail
www.manche-tourisme.com/medianet-uk.htm	Manche, France Tourist Site
www.metoffice.gov.uk/weather/uk/se/se_forecast_weather.html	Weather Forecast Hampshire
http://visitnormandy.org/Normandy.nsf/Visit/Meteo.htm	Weather Forecast Normandy
www.enjoyengland.com/	UK Tourist Office
www.yha.org.uk	British Youth Hostel Association
www.fuaj.org	French Youth Hostel Association
www.thelongridersguild.com/	Information resource for long riders
www.ecf.com/	EuroVelo, European cycle route network

Further Reading

The Pilgrim's France	James and Colleen Heater
The Art of Pilgrimage	Phil Cousineau
Have Saddle Will Travel	Don West
The Essential Walker's Journal	Leslie Sansone
Pilgrim Tales: On and Off the Road to Santiago	Nancy Frey

About General French Vocabulary

ENGLISH	FRENCH	ENGLISH	FRENCH
Sunday	dimanche	one	un
Monday	lundi	two	deux
Tuesday	mardi	three	trois
Wednesday	mercredi	four	quatre
Thursday	jeudi	five	cinq
Friday	vendredi	six	six
Saturday	samedi	seven	sept
January	janvier	eight	huit
February	février	nine	neuf
March	mars	ten	dix
April	avril	eleven	onze
May	mai	twelve	douze
June	juin	thirteen	treize
July	juillet	fourteen	quatorze
August	août	fifteen	quinze
September	septembre	sixteen	seize
October	octobre	seventeen	dix-sept
November	novembre	eighteen	dix-huit
December	décembre	nineteen	dix-neuf
today	aujourd'hui	twenty	vingt
yesterday	hier	thirty	trente
tomorrow	demain	forty	quarante
in the morning	le matin	fifty	cinquante
in the afternoon	l'après-midi	sixty	soixante
in the evening	le soir	seventy	soixante-dix
now	maintenant	seventy-five	soixante-quinze
later	plus tard	eighty	quatres-vingt
at midday	à midi	ninety	quatres-vingt-dix
at one o'clock	à une heure	one hundred	cent
bus	autobus, bus, car	on the other side of	à l'autre cote de
bus stop	arrêt	on the corner of	à l'angle de
bus station	gare routière	next to	à cote de
car	voiture	behind	derrière
train station	gare	in front of	devant
what time does it arrive/leave?	il arrive/part à quelle heure?	before	avant
how many kilometres	combien de kilomètres?	after	aprés
how many hours	combien d'heures?	under	sous
on foot	à pied	to cross	traverser
the road to	la route à	where?	ou?
near	prés/pas loin	when?	quand?
far	loin	how many/much?	combien?
left	à gauche	why?	pourquoi?
right	à droite	at what time?	a quelle heure?
straight on	tout droit	a room for one/two person/people	une chambre pour une/deux personnes

18

Cycling

ENGLISH	FRENCH	ENGLISH	FRENCH
to adjust	ajuster	to lower	baisser
axle	l'axe	mudguard	le garde-boue
ball bearing	le roulement à billes	pannier	le panier
battery	la pile	pedal	la pédale
bent	tordu	pump	la pompe
bicycle	le vélo	puncture	la crevaison
brake cable	le câble	to raise	relever
brakes	les freins	to repair	réparer
broken	cassé	saddle	la selle
bulb	l'ampoule	to screw	visser
chain	la chaine	spanner	la clef
to deflate	dégonfler	spoke	le rayon
frame	le cadre	to straighten	redresser
gears	les vitesses	stuck	coincé
grease	la graisse	tight	serré
handlebar	le guidon	toe clips	les cale-pieds
to inflate	gonfler	tyre	pneu
inner tube	la chambre à air	wheel	la roue

Equine

ENGLISH	FRENCH	ENGLISH	FRENCH
stud (to put in horse shoe)	un crampon	stirrup	etrier
mane	la crinière	saddle pad	tapis de selle
tail	la queue	brush	brosse
horse	cheval	hoof-picks	cure-pieds
mare	jument	horse shoe	fer
foal	poulain	helmet	bombe
gelding	hongre	hat	chapeau
stallion	entier / etalon	gloves	gants
head	tête	boots	bottes
eyes	yeux	walk	pas
ears	oreilles	trot	trot
nostril	naseau	canter	galop
withers	garrot	saddle	selle
croup (rear)	croupe	girth	sangle
neck	encolure	bridle	bride
to shorten	raccourcir	rope	longe
legs	jambes	to unsaddle	desseller
hoof	sabot	to girth	sangler
tack	harnachement (général)	to loosen the girth	dessangler
lame	boiter		

"Pilgrims are poets who create by taking journeys."

Richard R. Niebuhr

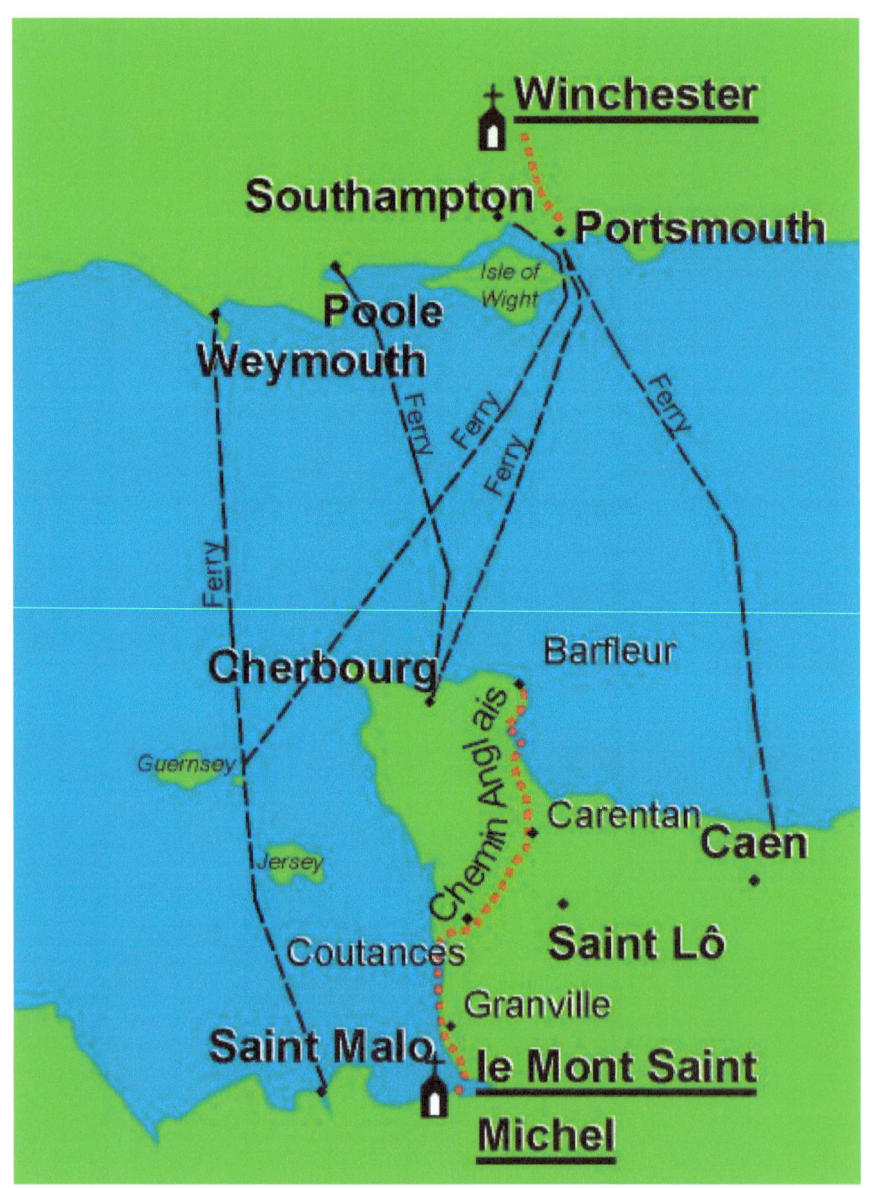

Many pilgrims would have started on what is today known as the Millenium Footpath Trail, a 155 mile long-distance footpath that connects Winchester Cathedral in Hampshire, England, to Mont St Michel in Normandy, France. The cult of St. Michael was widespread in the British Isles from the ninth century and by the time of the Reformation in the 16th century there were more than 600 churches in England dedicated to St. Michael. St Michael's day, Michelmas, is celebrated on 29 September. In France, the Norman sanctuary of Mont Saint Michel attracted pilgrims from Scandinavia, Italy and Germany, as well as from Britain.

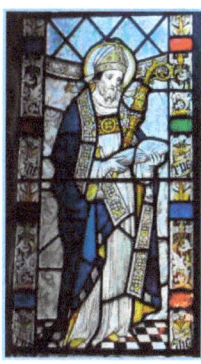

The Hampshire Millenium Pilgrims' Trail runs between Winchester and Portsmouth, through Bishop's Waltham. The Trail will take you on a journey through today's landscape, with a pilgrim's eyes. The medieval landscape is all around if you take the time and know where to look.

Getting There

Winchester is easily accessible by road and rail from all parts of Great Britain and the main airports, but of course not everyone will be starting from here. Information is also given within the guide for all other main access points along the route. Winchester station is 10 mins from the Cathedral. Trains run north to Basingstoke, Woking and London Waterloo and south to Portsmouth or to Southampton Airport, Southampton Central, Bournemouth and Weymouth.

Useful links and contacts for this section:

www.southwesttrains.co.uk

www.carlberry.co.uk

Winchester Railway Ticket Office   0845 6000 650
Ticket Office Hours:
Monday-Friday   06:00-20:30
Saturday   06:00-19:30
Sunday   07:00-20:30

Hampshire County Council, The Castle, Winchester, HampshireSO23 8UJ
Email: info.centres@hants.gov.uk
Free helpline for calls made within Hampshire   0800 028 0888
Calls from within the UK   01962 870500
Main switchboard   01962 841841
www3.hants.gov.uk/longdistance/pilgrim-trail.htm

Winchester Tourist Information Centre, Winchester Guildhall, High Street, Winchester SO23 9GH
Tel: 0044 (0)1962 840 500
www.visitwinchester.co.uk/

Winchester to Bishop's Waltham 18.1km

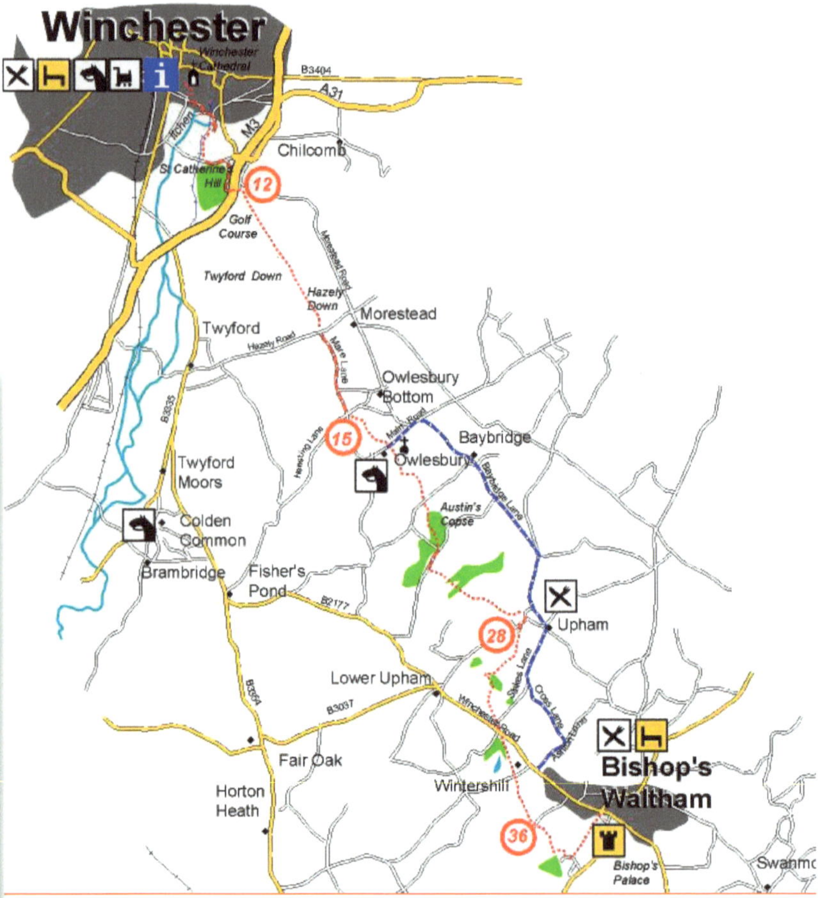

Winchester to Bishop's Waltham 18.1km

Route Summary: this section is largely undertaken on pathways following the course of a Roman Road across rolling and open country. Unfortunately there are many stiles on the route making it unsuitable for cyclists and horse-riders beyond Waypoint #16

Way Point	Distance	Directions	Verification Point	Compass
1		Facing the West door of the Cathedral turn right and proceed through the cloisters	South wall of cathedral	SE
2	70	Bear right to leave the cloisters and pass the Deanery on your left	Enter The Close	S
3	200	Pass beside Cheyney Court and leave the Close through the Priory Gate.	Enter St Swithun's Street	W
4	40	Immediately turn left to pass through King's Gate	Enter Kingsgate Street	SW
5	30	Turn left into College Street	Pass Winchester College on the right	SE
6	300	Road bears right and then left into College Walk	Initially beside College grounds and then along tree lined street	SE
7	300	Cross the river Itchen and turn right on Domum Road		SE
8	150	Take the second turning to the right to follow the path beside the canalised - Itchen River		S
9	800	At the bridge leave the canal-side and turn left on Garnier Road		E
10	500	Just before reaching the roundabout turn right on Morestead Road	Proceed with motorway on the left	S
11	300	Continue straight ahead parallel to the motorway and cross the footbridge over the M3	St Catherine's Hill to the right	S
12	250	After the bridge turn right onto the long straight track crossing open ground	Motorway and golf course to the right	SE
13	2300	Continue straight ahead beside line of trees and War Memorial		S
14	500	At crossroads go straight ahead	Mare Lane	S
15	1500	At crossroads with Hensting Lane and Hatcher's Lane go straight ahead then immediately bear left on the path diagonally across the field		SE

Winchester to Bishop's Waltham 18.1km

Winchester to Bishop's Waltham 18.1km

Way Point	Distance	Directions	Verification Point	Compass
16	900	At the T-junction with Main Road in Owlesbury turn right and immediately left into the church yard. **Note:-** the track ahead involves steps and numerous stiles. Cyclists and horse riders may avoid these by turning left on Main Road and then taking the first right – Baybridge Lane – to the village of Upham and then onwards via Shoe Lane, Stakes Lane, Cross Lane and Ashton Lane to Bishop's Waltham and the end of the section	St Andrew's church	SE
17	100	Diagonally cross the church yard and exit via the steps and bear right into Pitcot Lane		SE
18	1000	At the bottom of the hill go straight ahead across Lower Baybridge Lane	Gravel track	S
19	300	Continue straight ahead towards the copse of trees	Path keeps initially to the right side of the copse	S
20	600	Emerge from the copse and bear right onto track keeping the copse on your right and open fields to the left		SW
21	400	Turn left across open fields	Monarch's Way towards the village of Upham	SE
22	900	Cross the stile in the hedge and bear left, diagonally crossing next field	Towards copse	E
23	200	Continue straight ahead crossing 2 lines of trees and emerging on a grass track		SE
24	300	Take the left fork across the field		E
25	300	Beside the trees turn left and then bear right towards the road and the centre of Upham		E

Way Point	Distance	Directions	Verification Point	Compass
26	160	On meeting the road turn right	Upham Street	S
27	90	At the road junction in the centre of Upham, bear right remaining on Upham Street	Church on the left	SW
28	140	Turn left on Oak Close		S
29	80	Bear left on the pathway		S
30	300	At junction with the broader track bear right	Towards trees	SW
31	600	Bear right and skirt the woods keeping them to your left		S
32	400	At the end of the woods, bear right across the field towards the main road		S
33	600	At junction with a minor road cross straight over and follow the road ahead	Stakes Lane	S
34	180	At the intersection with the Winchester Road cross over to take the footpath ahead	Pond visible on the right as you pass through the trees	S
35	700	At crossroads, cross over Winters Hill and bear right on the path keeping the Nursery to your left	Woodlea Nurseries	SE
36	900	Cross farm road and continue straight ahead	Tangier farm to the right	SE
37	600	Turn left and then bear right keeping trees on your right	Passing beside Brooklands Farm	E
38	200	At intersection with the farm road turn left		E
39	110	Take the left fork onto the disused railway track	Towards the centre of Bishop's Waltham	NE
40	800	Arrive at the roundabout in Bishop's Watham	Bishop's Palace to the right	

Winchester to Bishop's Waltham 18.1km

Accommodation	Price	Opening	Animals
The King Alfred Pub, Saxon Road SO23 7DJ WINCHESTER Tel: 0044 (0)1962 854370	B2	All Year	
Somerville, 19 Bereweeke Way WINCHESTER SO22 6BJ Tel: 0044 (0)1962 850979	B2	All Year	
First In, Last Out, 37 Wales Street WINCHESTER SO23 0ET Tel: 0044 (0)1962 865963	B2	All Year	
PANORAMIC VIEWS, 16 West End Terrace WINCHESTER SO22 5EN Tel: 0044 (0)7760 477531 Mobile: 0044 (0)7760 477531	B2	All Year	
Orchard House, Manor Road Twyford WINCHESTER SO21 1RJ Tel: 0044 (0)7786654166	B2	All Year	
The House on the Hill BISHOPS WALTHAM SO32 1FH Tel: 0044 (0)1489892431 Mobile: 0044 (0)777 6302446	B2	All Year	
Post Mead, Shore Lane BISHOP'S WALTHAM SO32 1DY Tel: 0044 (0)1489 895795	B1	All Year	

Equestrian Centre

Owslebury Equestrian Centre, Owslebury WINCHESTER SO21 1JN
Tel: 0044 (0)1962 777453

Southfield Equestrian Centre, Southfield Farm, Micheldever Rd WHITCHURCH
RG28 7JL Tel: 0044 (0)1256 896859

Useful Contacts

Tourist Offices

Tourist Information Centre, Winchester Guildhall, High Street WINCHESTER SO23 9GH Tel: 0044 (0)1962 840 500 tourism@winchester.gov.uk
www.visitwinchester.co.uk/site/home

Internet Cafe

Mailboxes Etc, 80 High Street WINCHESTER SO23 9AT Tel: 0044 (0)1962 622 133

Copyman , 11 Charlecote Mews, Staple Gardens WINCHESTER SO23 8SR
Tel: 0044 (0)1962 863 105 repro@copyman-online.co.uk
www.copyman_online.co.uk

Doctor

St. Clements Partnership, Tanner Street WINCHESTER SO23 8AD
Tel: 0044 (0)1962 852211

Veterinary

Companion Care Vet Surgery, Unit 2 Easton Lane WINCHESTER SO23 7XA
Tel: 0044 (0)1962 843885

Winchester is at the western end of the South Downs with the scenic River Itchen running through it and a number of famous historic buildings dominating the skyline. Winchester Cathedral, originally built in 1079, is the second longest cathedral in Europe. It also houses the shrine of Saint Swithun and is the beginning of the ancient Pilgrims' Way leading to Canterbury, making it an important pilgrim centre. The cathedral houses much fine architecture spanning the 11th to the 16th century and is the burial place for numerous Bishops and later monarchs such as King Canute and William Rufus. The writer, Jane Austen, is also buried here. **Winchester Castle** is best known for its Great Hall (built sometime between 1222-1235) and famous for King Arthur's Round Table, which has hung in the hall from at least 1463. The names of the legendary Knights of the

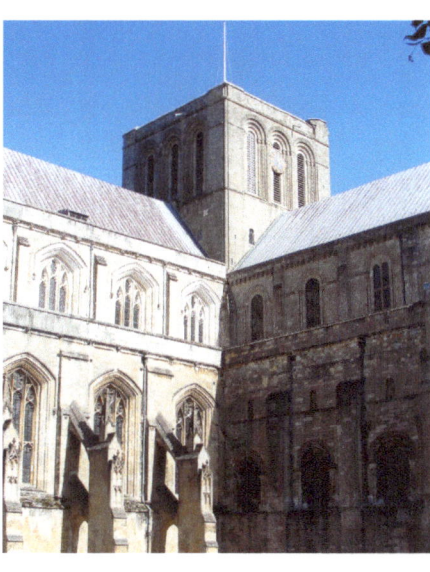

Round Table are written around the edge of the table surmounted by King Arthur on his throne. **Winchester College** is a public school founded in 1832 by William of Wykeham for the education of poor boys before they moved on to New College, Oxford and a life in the church. There are two courtyards, a gatehouse, cloister, hall, a magnificent college chapel and also The Water Meadows, which have a part of the River Itchen running through them.

The name, **Bishop's Waltham** is comprised of three parts: 'walt' - forest; 'ham' - settlement'; and 'Bishop's'. Local residents often refer to the town simply as 'Waltham', which is reasonable

enough as there is no longer a Bishop in residence. If you have the time, try to stop off here for at least a few hours. Bishop's Waltham started life as a Saxon village, and steadily grew to become one of Hampshire's larger settlements, despite being burnt to the ground by Danes in 1001 AD. By the time of the Domesday Book (1086 AD), it had a population of around 450. In 904, it was given by the King to the Bishop of Winchester. In 1136 Henry de Blois, a later bishop built Bishop's Waltham Palace, destroyed on the orders of William Cromwell during the English Civil war. Apart from the ruins, which are open to the public and well worth a visit, material from the Palace was used as building materials in town buildings still standing to this day. In addition there are many Georgian buildings in the town, alongside the Norman parish church of St Peter.

Geography
Good news for anyone planning to follow this section of the route; the terrain in Hampshire is predominantly undulating and its very highest (Pilot Hill - not on your route), rises to no more than 286 m (938 ft).

Climate
Hampshire has a milder climate than most areas of the British Isles, being in the far south with the climate stabilising effect of the sea, but protected against the more extreme weather of the Atlantic coast. Nevertheless, you can expect rainfall at anytime.

Flora and Fauna
In Hampshire, like the rest of England, hundreds of species of wildflowers bloom from spring to autumn - from rare varieties of orchid, saxifrage and mountain pansy to the primroses, violets and bluebells that are found in many a woodland clearing. The names of some of the less common species are quite enchanting - fairy flax, cottongrass and yellow wort, ragged-robin, muscatel and tormentil. Depending on the time of year, you are bound to see at least some of these. The Pilgrim Trail takes you through the Forest of Bere, a mixture of woodland, open space, heathland, farmland and downland which is important to many different people for a variety of reasons. Together with the remaining 19th century oak and modern 20th century conifer plantations, there are areas of retained scrub and coppice, streams, ponds and an extensive network of rides and paths. The many habitats provide an excellent area for nature lovers, whatever the season.

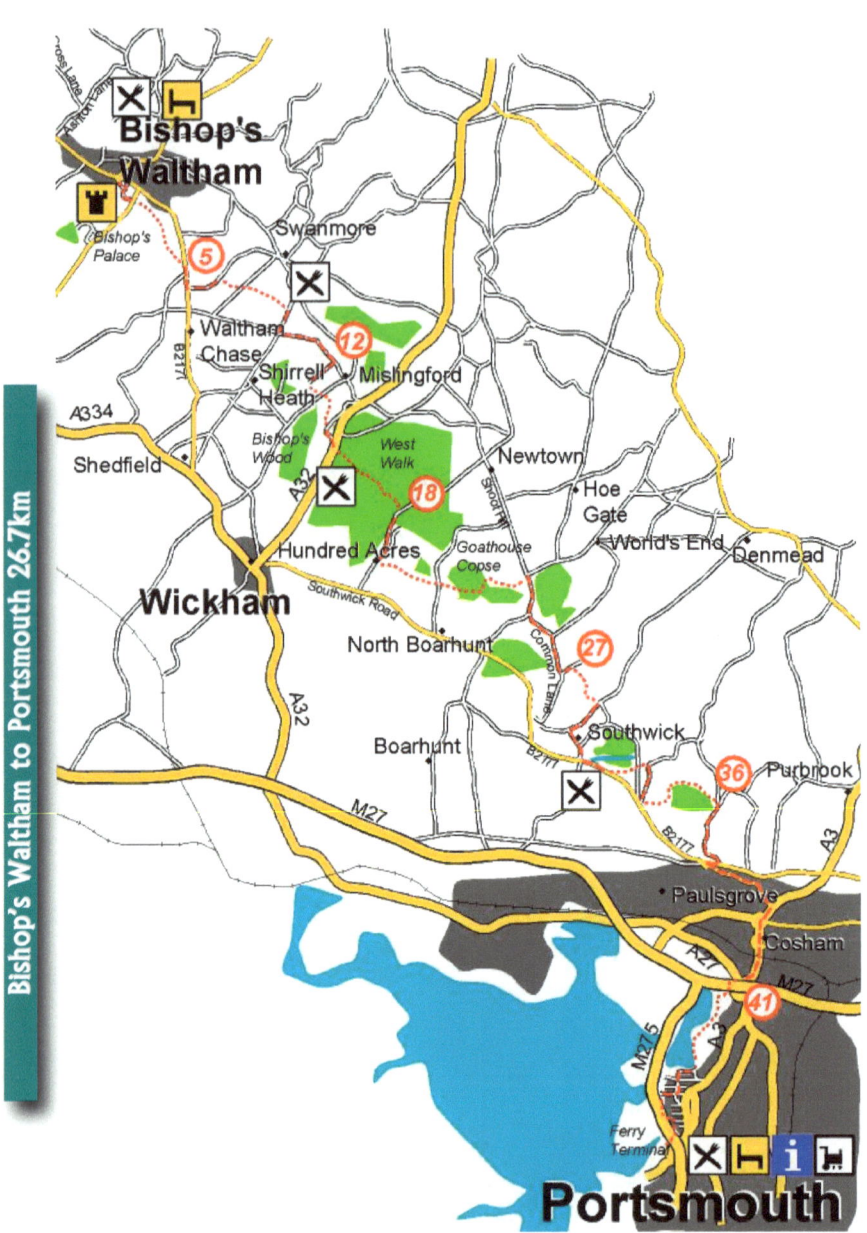

Route Summary: this section is both long and strenuous. Pathways and woodland tracks dominate initially with increasing use of roads on the approach to Portsmouth. In Portsmouth a cycle track helps avoid the busiest roads on the final approach to the ferry terminal.

Way Point	Distance	Directions	Verification Point	Compass
1		From the roundabout on Winchester Road in Bishop's Waltham take exit to Station Road		SE
2	200	Turn right and skirt the ruins of the Bishop's Palace	Bishop's Lane, keep ruins to the left	SE
3	300	At T-junction with Botley Road, cross over and take the path ahead		SE
4	1400	At the intersection with the main road turn right and proceed on the grass verge		S
5	500	At the crossroads turn left	Lower Chase Road	E
6	400	At fork bear left	Remain on Lower Chase Road	NE
7	150	Just after bridge turn right onto path		SE
8	400	Cross over New Road and take the gravelled track	The Lakes	SE
9	800	At T-junction turn right	Gravel Hill	SW
10	400	At crossroads turn left	Bishop's Wood Road	E
11	600	Remain on the road and bear right	Woods to the left	SE
12	400	Turn right	Towards Hawk's Nest Farm	SW
13	500	Turn to the left remaining on the road		SE
14	300	Cross Newman's Hill and take the footpath ahead	Keep the wood, Bishop's Wood, to right	S
15	300	After crossing the river bear left away from the woods	Towards Kingsmead farm	S
16	300	Turn right on Kingsmead Road	Beside farm entrance	S
17	400	Cross the very busy A32 onto the path into the forest	West Walk	SE
18	1700	At the junction with Hundred Acres Road turn right		SW
19	800	At the end of the brick wall turn left on the path	Pass beside Little Forest	E
20	1200	On reaching Trampers Lane turn right and almost immediately left over the stile	North Boarhunt	E
21	600	Turn left further into the woods	Goathouse Copse	NE
22	200	Bear right and continue with woods on your right		E
23	700	At junction with Shoot Hill turn sharp right	Shoothill Lodge	S
24	600	Take the left fork	Common Lane	SE

Bishop's Waltham to Portsmouth 26.7km

Way Point	Distance	Directions	Verification Point	Compass
25	600	Continue straight ahead on Common Lane	Avoid Beckford Lane turning	S
26	400	Turn left towards Vernon's Farm		E
27	200	Bear right onto the path	Before reaching Mitchelland	SE
28	800	At junction with road turn right on Back Lane	Towards Southwick	SW
29	500	Turn left on Southwick High Street	Pass church	S
30	500	At roundabout turn left and remain on the left side of the road	Southwick Park Lake to the left	SE
31	500	Bear left on the path beside golf course		E
32	500	At crossroads in track go straight ahead		E
33	160	At junction turn right on Pitymoor Lane		S
34	500	At the intersection with the major road turn sharp left onto the path towards the woods	B2177 Southwick Road	E
35	400	Bear left into the edge of the woods		N
36	1200	handlebar	Climb the hill on the road passing the entrance to Pigeon House Farm	S
37	1400	At T-junction turn right on Portsdown Road	Towards roundabout	W
38	200	At roundabout turn sharp left and descend the hill on Southwick Hill Road		SE
39	1500	At the T-junction turn right on London Road		SW
40	300	At the roundabout continue straight ahead on Northern Road crossing a second roundabout		S
41	1000	At the third roundabout beside the M27 pass around the right-hand side of the roundabout	Cycle track and pathway	SW
42	200	Turn right onto the cycle track	Hillsea Creek immediately to the right	SW
43	1900	Turn left on Twyford Avenue	Just after passing Sports Centre	S
44	80	Turn right towards the Greyhound Stadium		W

Way Point	Distance	Directions	Verification Point	Compass
45	200	Turn left on Target Road		S
46	150	At the T-junction turn right on Tipner Road		W
47	40	Turn left on Widley Road		S
48	130	At the second crossroads turn right on Jervis Road		W
49	190	Turn left on the pathway through the park	Parallel to the motorway – M275	S
50	300	Go straight ahead across the car park and bear right on the road	Closer to the motorway	SE
51	180	Bear right on the pathway between the houses and the motorway		SE
52	300	At the roundabout turn right and take the underpass	Rudmore Roundabout	SW
53	70	Carefully cross the motorway slip road and bear left towards the ferry terminal		SW
54	120	Arrive at the Portsmouth Ferry Terminal		

Accommodation	Price	Opening	Animals
Hamilton House Bed & Breakfast, 95 Victoria Rd North SOUTHSEA PO5 1PS Tel 0044 (0)23 92823502 www.hamiltonhouse.co.uk	B2	All Year	
44 Waverley Road PORTSMOUTH PO5 2PP Tel: 0044 (0)23 92811337 enquiries@birchwood.uk.com **Note:** No single nights available over the weekend	B2	All Year	
23 Victoria Road South SOUTHSEA PO5 2BX Tel: 0044 (0)23 92811157 bookings@lamornaguesthouse.co.uk	B2	All Year	

Youth Hostel	Price	Opening	Animals
Portsmouth and Southsea Backpackers Lodge, 4 Florence Road, Southsea PORTSMOUTH PO5 2NE Tel: 44 (0)23 92832495 info@portsmouthbackpackers.co.uk www.portsmouthbackpackers.co.uk	B1	All Year	

Equestrian Centre,
Fort Widley Equestrian Centre, Portsmouth, PO6 3LS Tel: 0044 (0)23 92324553

Bishop's Waltham to Portsmouth 26.7km

Useful Contacts

Tourist Offices
Portsmouth Tourist Information Centre, The Hard PORTSMOUTH
PO1 3QJ Tel: 0044 (0)23 92826722 www.visitportsmouth.co.uk/

Internet Cafes
Net Cafe, 4 Market Way PORTSMOUTH PO1 4BX
Tel: 0044 (0)23 92864455

Jamocha Cafe Ltd, 99 Elm Grove SOUTHSEA PO5 1LH
Tel: 0044 (0)23 92875000

Online Cafe, 163 Elm Gro SOUTHSEA PO5 1LU Tel: 0044 (0)23 92831106

Cyber Cafe, 1c Albert Rd SOUTHSEA PO5 2SE Tel: 0044 (0)23 92864158

Peace Cafe, 59 Castle Rd SOUTHSEA PO5 3AY Tel: 0044 (0)23 92830544

Doctor
Lake Road Practice, Nutfield Place PORTSMOUTH PO1 4JT
Tel: 0044 (0)844 4773540

Veterinary
Harbour Veterinary Group, 251 London Road, North End PORTSMOUTH PO2 9HA
Tel: 0044 (0)23 92484788

Portsmouth has been a significant naval port for centuries, boasts the world's oldest dry dock still in use and is home to many famous ships, including Nelson's famous flagship HMS Victory. The Royal Navy's reliance on Portsmouth led to the city becoming the most fortified in Europe with a network of forts circling the city. Portsmouth has declined as a military port in recent years but remains a major dockyard and base for the Royal Navy. There is also a commercial port serving destinations on the continent for freight and passenger traffic. The Spinnaker Tower, a recent addition to the city's skyline, can be found in the recently re-developed area known as Gunwharf Quays.

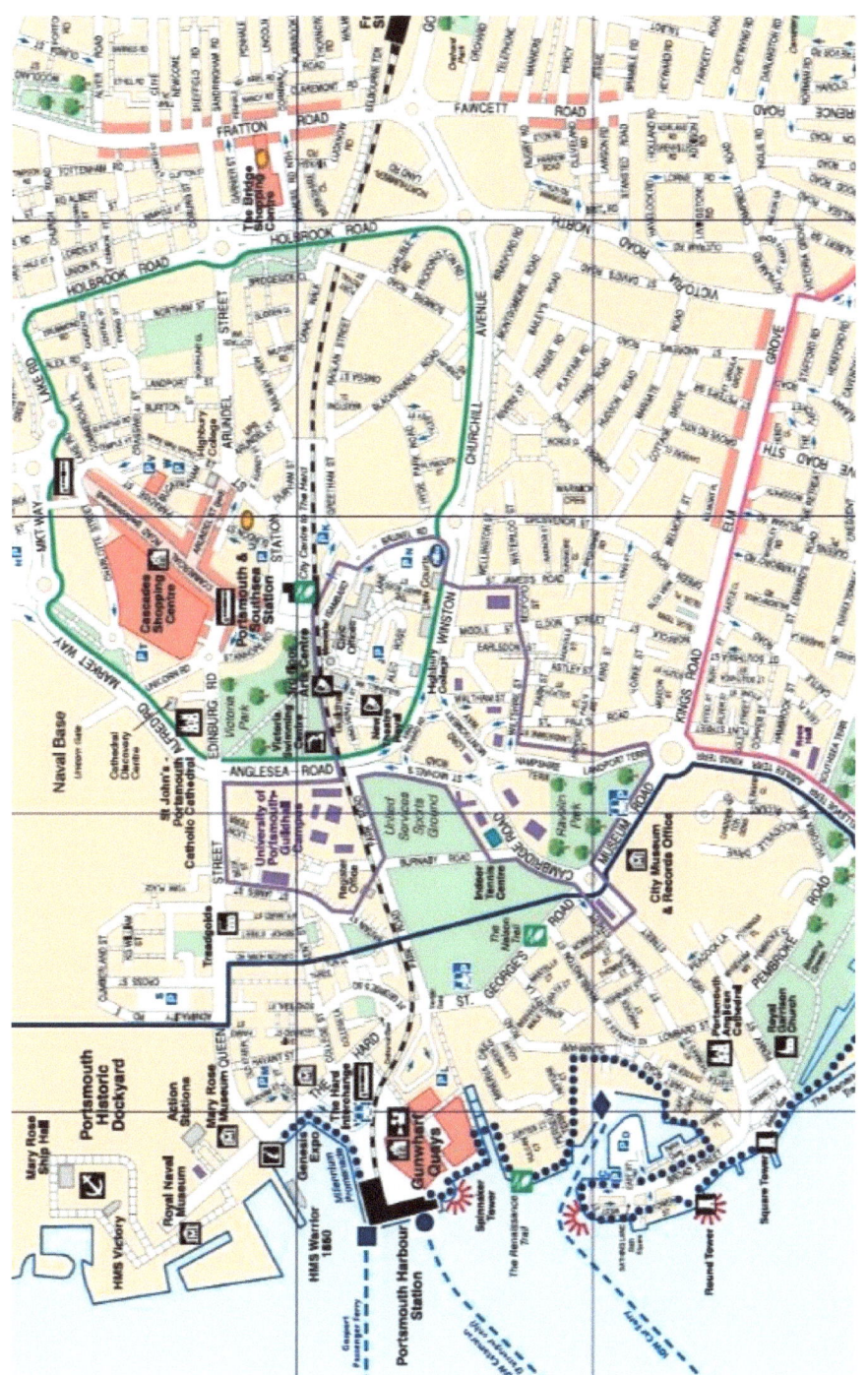

PORTSMOUTH - CHERBOURG FERRY OPERATORS

Brittany Ferries 11 crossings weekly, 2h 45min sailing
Brittany Ferries, The Brittany Centre, Wharf Rd, Portsmouth, PO2 8RU
Tel: 0044 870 536 0360   www.brittany-ferries.com
Note: this is the latest information at the time of publication, but will need to be verified.

Portsmouth to Barfleur

Month	Outbound			Inbound			Price Each way
	Dates	Time	Day	Dates	Time	Day	
April	01/04/08 - 10/07/08	08:00	Mon - Sun	01/04/08 - 10/07/08	17:30	Mon - Sun	
May	Exc. 23/05 - 29/05 & 16/06/08	08:15	Exc. Saturdays	Exc. 22/05 & 26/05 - 31/05 1, 16, 18/06 & 02/07/08	20:15	Exc. Sat	£76.00
June		15:45					
July							
August	8/7/08	15:45	Thurs	8/12/08	20:15	Tues	£92.00
September	9/7/08	15:45	Sun	9/12/08	20:15	Fri	£76.00
October	06/10/08 - 23/10/08 Exc. 11/10 & 18/10/08	08:15 or 15:45	Daily	13/10/08 - 26/10/08 Exc. 18/10 & 25/10/08	17:30 or 20:15	Daily	£58.00

Condor Ferries 1 crossing weekly, 5h 30min sailing
Condor Ferries Ltd, Continental Ferryport, George Byng Way, Portsmouth, PO2 8QN

Sailing dates	Portsmouth	Cherbourg		Portsmouth
Sundays from 25th May to 7th September	depart 0930	arrive 1600	depart 1700	arrive 2100

Tel: 0044 (0)23 92664676   www.condorferries.co.uk

Cherbourg is in the Manche *département*, in the Basse-Normandie region and has a varied history. During the Napoleonic era the harbour was fortified to prevent British naval incursions. Underwater obstructions were sunk at intervals across the harbour entrance, and then progressively replaced with piles of rubble. The port was also the first stop for RMS Titanic after it left Southampton, England. In 1944, the Battle of Cherbourg followed the Normandy Invasion, which ended with the capture of Cherbourg. Aside from its somewhat chequered history, Cherbourg does not appear to have much to offer today, and your authors recommend that after disembarking from the ferry, you head straight out of the town and look for a more picturesque place to take your first break.

Getting to Barfleur from Cherbourg

The starting point for the route in France is Barfleur, 25 kilometres east of Cherbourg.

Barfleur was the biggest port in Normandy seven centuries ago and suffered from being the favoured port of the English in the Middle-Ages. In 1120 Prince William, the only son of Henry I, drowned when his ship sank just off Barfleur harbour. Then in 1348, the town was burned by Edward III and again by a sequence of invaders during the 15th and 16th centuries. Most of the houses seen around the town and port were constructed in the 17th and 18th centuries, when the town was prosperous due to fishing. Since then the population has dwindled and fortunes have diminished - most recently through the invasion of a strain of plankton that poisoned all the mussels. Now all that remains is a pleasant port supported by fishing and oyster harvesting, but still relatively undisturbed by tourist activity.

Bus Service (Trains to Barfleur run only from Valognes, a distance of 27 km from Cherbourg).

Departure Cherbourg (Bus Station)	Arrival Barfleur (Le Port - Bar PMU)	Days	Bus Number	Service - School Holidays	Service - School Term
12.30	13.15	Mon - Fri	105	No	Yes
12.30	13.15	Mon - Fri	103	Yes	No
17.35	18.20	Mon - Fri	107	No	Yes
18.05	18.50	Mon - Fri	113	No	Yes
18.30	19.42	Mon, Tues, Thurs, Fri	109	Yes	No

Accommodation	Price	Opening	Animals
Citotel Hôtel Beauséjour, 26 Rue Grande Vallée 50100 CHERBOURG Tel: 0033 (0)02 33 53 10 30	B2	All Year	🐴
9, rue des Vieilles Carrieres, C/O Jean-Claude Cloarec 50100 CHERBOURG Tel: 0033 (0)2 33 94 61 67 cloarec.jean-claude@orange.fr	B2	All Year	🚫
Hotel le Moderne, 1 Place du General de Gaulle 50760 BARFLEUR Tel: 0033 (0)2 33 23 91 58	B2	All Year	🐴
Hotel le Conquerant, 16 rue St Thomas Becket 50760 BARFLEUR Tel: 0033 (0)2 33 54 00 82	B2	All Year	🐴
Maison de Fourmi, 16 rue de la Halle 50760 BARFLEUR Tel: 0033 (0)2 33 43 78 74	B2	All Year	🐴
Les Transats, 11 Quai Henri Chardon 50760 BARFLEUR Tel: 0033 (0)2 33 43 77 29 Mobile: 0033 (0)6 08 15 78 85	B2	All Year	🐴
Mme Me Roulier, rue de la Planque 50760 BARFLEUR Tel: 0033 (0)2 33 23 93 75	B2	All Year	🐴

Youth Hostel	Price	Opening	Animals
55, rue de l'Abbaye 50100 CHERBOURG Tel: 0033 (0)233781515 cherbourg@fuaj.org	B1	All Year	🚫

Camping	Price	Opening	Animals
INDIANA, 21 r Réville 50760 BARFLEUR Tel: 0033 (0)2 33 23 95 61 phlefe@yahoo.fr www.camping-indiana.com	B1	23 June - 10 Sept	🐴
LA BLANCHE NEF Tel: 0033 (0)2 33 23 15 40 Lablanchenef@wanadoo.fr www.lablanchenef.com	B1	All Year	🐴

Equestrian Centre
Centre Equestre du Douet Picot, 8 cha Guillard 50110 DIGOSVILLE Tel: 0033 (0)2 33 22 50 94 **Note:** 7.5 km from Cherbourg

Useful Contacts

Tourist Offices
Maison Tourisme Cherbourg Haut Cotentin, 2 quai Alexandre III 50100 CHERBOURG OCTEVILLE Tel: 0033 (0)2 33 93 52 02 www.otcherbourgcotentin.fr/

2, Rond Point le Conquérant, 50 760 BARFLEUR Tel: 0033 (0)2 33 54 02 48
office.tourisme.barfleur@wanadoo.fr www.ville-barfleur.fr

Internet Cafes
Archesys, 16 r de L'Union 50100 CHERBOURG Tel: 0033 0(2) 33 53 04 93
eric@endelin.com

Doctor
Godefroy Carine, 9 r Magenta 50100 CHERBOURG Tel: 0033 (0)2 33 53 25 05

Talbourdet Vincent, 34 quai Henri Chardon 50760 BARFLEUR
Tel: 0033 (0)2 33 43 24 00

Veterinary
Clinique Vétérinaire Docteurs Hamel et Lecanu, 13 r Paul Doumer 50100 CHERBOURG
Tel: 0033 (0)2 33 53 51 40

Farrier
Mouchel Marc, 12 Bis ham Bellanville 50330 COSQUEVILLE
Tel: 0033 (0)2 33 54 67 94

Geography - the Normandy west coast is sheltered from the east and north winds and benefits from the warm currents of the Gulf Stream. Here, 100 kilometres of sand unfold like a long ribbon. The sunniest beaches are here and the sea is a beautiful shade of deep blue. Inland, the greater part of the route will be along relatively flat coastal plains without too much in the way of tough ascents or descents.

Climate - since Normandy is on the north coast of France, it has a warm temperate climate. It does rain sometimes, which is one of the reasons its countryside is so green and wooded. It can get pretty hot in the summer months, up to about 30 degrees, but unlike France south of the Loire, you are unlikely to get scorched to the tarmac. Overall Normandy has an ideal climate for walking, cycling or riding, but bring waterproofs as well as a sunhat!

Flora and Fauna - thousands of years ago The Normandy Contentin peninsula was an island. Now it boasts some of the best coastline in the region; long sandy beaches, rugged coastal walks. The estuaries of numerous rivers — Vire, Taute, Douve and Aure on the eastern side, are surrounded by a rich variety of habitat: fenland, marsh, water-meadow, estuary, pinewood, dunes and bocage (the typical Norman countryside of small fields surrounded by hedgerows). If you start to feel weary, you can distract yourself by looking out for the seals in the Baie des Veys near Carentan and Isigny, and above all, thousands of birds: teal, waders, oyster-catchers, curlew, buzzards, tern, storks, and migratory birds of all kinds.

Several centuries ago **Barfleur** was the largest port in Normandy, famous for the night of 25th November 1120 when the ship carrying Prince William to England struck a rock causing the death of the heir to the English throne and chaos in the monarchy. Later, the town was burned down by Edward III in 1348 and then again during the 15th and 16th centuries. In 1692 the Battle of Barfleur took place just off the coast. Today, Barfleur is simply an attractive and active fishing port, dominated by the Church of St Nicholas, probably best known for its 17th century statue of St Roch, patron saint of dogs.

Look out For: Croix Odin, on Pointe de Landemer after Barfleur

Route Summary: the section generally follows the Sentier Littoral and GR223 along the Noth East coast of the Contentin Peninsula. The terrain is generally flat and in good weather this makes for easy walking and riding. Some diversions are suggested for cyclists to avoid loose sand.

Look out for: Reville parish church with 15th century hapel of St James.

Way Point	Distance	Directions	Verification Point	Compass
1		From the Church of St Nicolas, situated at the northern end of the harbour, turn right along the harbour-side in the direction of the town centre	Quai Henri Chardon	S
2	700	Bear left turn onto a gravel track behind a group of houses. At the end of the gravel tack turn left onto a short section of road	Rue Pierre Salley	E
3	160	At the T-junction turn left. **Note:-** Cyclists may prefer to avoid the soft sand on the coastal path and turn right to take the D1 and rejoin the route at Way Point #12	Rue Julie Poste	N
4	90	Turn right on rue du 24 mai 1944		NE
5	200	Turn right to follow the grassy track as it runs south along the top of the cliff	Chemin du Mont Saint Michel sign	S
6	400	Go straight across the car-park and follow the small path beside the sea		SE
7	1500	At the edge of a field, turn left onto the beach and back up again		SE
8	300	Straight ahead passing a Sentier Littoral sign post	Le Cap 0. 8 kilometres	SE
9	300	Straight ahead passing the Pointe de Moulard	Ruins of La Tour de Moulard in the sea	S
10	400	The track emerges onto a small gravel road where you turn right	Sign-post to Landemer	W
11	200	Pass through le Cap on the outskirts of the village of Landemer	Bay to the left	SW
12	200	At the crossroads turn left	D1	S
13	200	After a very short section of the D1 bear left and leave the road	Chemin du Mont Saint Michel sign	S
14	500	Turn sharp left down a grassy track	Returning towards the sea	SE
15	700	The track emerges onto a minor road, turn left. Remain parallel to the sea shore	Cormorants can often be seen on the rocks.	S
16	500	Take the right fork	Caravan park to the left	W
17	500	At the T-junction, with a minor road, turn left		S
18	600	Leave the road to take a track to the right	Chemin du Mont Saint Michel sign	SW

Barfleur to Saint-Vaast-la-Hougue 13.3km

41

Way Point	Distance	Directions	Verification Point	Compass
19	200	The track comes to an end, turn right on the road	La Baronnerie	W
20	140	After a very short distance take a left turn on the crown of the bend		SW
21	180	The minor road leads into a track, go straight ahead		S
22	300	At the end of the track, turn right onto a road		W
23	400	At T-junction, turn left onto route de Montey	Village of Réville	SW
24	300	Bear left in the direction of the camping and Jonville		SW
25	120	At the T-junction turn right	Rue d'Eglise	W
26	60	Take the left fork	Church of St Martin	W
27	100	Turn left along rue Général de Gaulle	Direction Saint-Vaast-la-Hougue	S
28	400	Bear left remaining on the D1		SE
29	400	Bear right to take the river bridge	La Saire	S
30	160	Just after the bridge take a left turn onto a gravel track. **Note:-** Cyclists should remain on the D1 until reaching Saint-Vaast-la-Hougue	Towards the sea	S
31	3100	Arrive in Saint-Vaast-la-Hougue beside the harbour	Restaurants and Tourist Office to the right	

Barfleur to Saint-Vaast-la-Hougue 13.3km

Accommodation	Price	Opening	Animals
Cottebrune Alain et Patricia, 16 rte Monts 50760 REVILLE Tel: 0033 (0)2 33 23 19 12	B2	All Year	🐎
La Granitiere, 74 rue Maréchal Foch 50550 SAINT VAAST LA HOUGUE Tel: 0033 (0)2 33 54 58 99 contact@hotel-la-granitiere.com www.hotel-la-granitiere.com	B3	All Year	🐎
CAFE DO PORT, 5 quai Vauban 50550 SAINT VAAST LA HOUGUE Tel: 0033 (0)2 33 23 42 42 www.cafe-du-port.com	B3	All Year	🐎
Mme Marie Christine RAISON, 1, rue Arisitide Briand 50550 SAINT VAAST LA HOUGUE Tel: 0033 (0)2 33 54 78 42 marie-christine.raison@wanadoo.fr	B2	All Year	🐎

Camping	Price	Opening	Animals
LA GALOUETTE, Tel: 0033 (0)2 33 54 20 57 contact@camping-lagallouette.fr www. lagallouette.com	B1	1 April - 30 Sept	🐎

Equestrian Centre
Poney Club du Val de Saire, 40 rte Monts 50760 REVILLE Tel: 0033 (0)2 33 23 13 37

Useful Contacts
Tourist Offices
1, place Général de Gaulle 50550 SAINT-VAAST-LA-HOUGUE
Tel: 0033 (0)2 33 23 19 32 office-de-tourisme@saint-vaast-reville.com
www.saint-vaast-reville.com

Doctor
Poulet François, 119 r Mar Foch 50550 SAINT VAAST LA HOUGUE
Tel: 0033 (0)2 33 54 41 45

Barfleur to Saint-Vaast-la-Hougue 13.3km

Route Summary: the section continues by following the Sentier Littoral and GR223 before turning inland to begin crossing the peninsula. Alternatives are offered for riders and cyclists to avoid steps and wicket gates.

44

Way Point	Distance	Directions	Verification Point	Compass
1		From the harbour-side in Saint-Vaast-la-Hougue, continue south along the harbour on Quai de Tourville, passing the harbour entrance to your left. **Note**:- to avoid numerous obstructions, horse-riders and cyclists should take the D1, direction Quettehou, and after 1.7 km turn left in the direction of le Carvallon and rejoin the route at Way Point #12	Île Tatihou to the left and pass by large anchor	SE
2	500	Continue on the sea wall with the open sea immediately to the left and the town to your right		W
3	110	Turn right and descend a flight of steps into a narrow alley and immediately turn left	Beside and below the sea-wall	SW
4	300	Turn right on a small grassy path between a caravan and camping site and the oyster beds of le Crau	The bay is home to an array of interesting birds, while there are great views of the Fort of la Hougue.	NW
5	300	Turn right onto a gravel path beside the campsite	Leaving the bay behind you	N
6	100	At the end of the track turn left on a minor road	Rue de la Gallouette	NW
7	40	Turn sharp right and then left	Rue d'Isamberville	NW
8	70	At fork bear left	Beside oyster processing factory	W
9	300	Bear left onto rue de Morsalines		W
10	140	Return to the beach, where the path takes you up a flight of steps and progressively narrows	Sea to the left	W
11	300	Straight ahead across a patch of tarmac. The path continues via a flight of steps		W
12	300	The track leads onto a minor road take the left and follow the chemin de la Bonde	Alternate route and route du Carvallon joins from right	SW
13	400	Turn left onto a grassy track	Remaining beside sea	SW
14	60	Take the footbridge over le Vaupreux. **Note**:- the bridge is impassable for horses but there is a water crossing		W
15	180	Turn left onto track		SW
16	80	At T-junction turn right	House ahead - Anais	NW

Saint-Vaast-la-Hougue to le Bourg de Lestre 11.9km

Way Point	Distance	Directions	Verification Point	Compass
17	60	Directly after the second house take a left. There is a small wicket gate and a flight of steps. **Note**:- riders avoid the left turn and continue for 700 metres before turning left onto the D14 for 1.9 kilometres and again turning left towards the sea and returning to the main path near the farm - le Triolet - at Way Point #30		SW
18	300	Cross a small launching area and after a wicket gate walk proceed along the end of a garden	Sign post showing the direction to la Redoute and le Carvallon	SW
19	160	After another wicket gate at the end of the garden, turn right on a minor road	Large house ahead	NW
20	150	Turn sharp left up a flight of steps beside a group of modern houses		SW
21	130	At the end of a small track cross over the minor road and go straight ahead up another flight of steps		SW
22	180	Pass through kissing gate and bear left		SE
23	70	Take a sharp left and then on a few metres before a sharp right.		SE
24	40	Through another wicket gate and take a sharp right and enter a group of houses	Le Rivage	S
25	70	Within the hamlet take the right fork		W
26	130	Turn left onto a gravel road	Red and white GR223 symbols	S
27	190	Pass through another kissing gate		SE
28	40	Turn sharp right just after a footbridge	Sea-shore close on the left	SW
29	200	Turn sharp left and skirt around the outside of a field		S
30	600	Straight ahead along a broad gravelled track beside the sea. **Note**:- riders and cyclists rejoin from the right		S
31	5000	Leave the coastal track and take the road to your right. **Note**:- for Quinéville remain on the GR223 coastal track for 1.5 km, rejoining the main route via the D421 to le Bourg de Lestre	Wooden Chemin St Michel sign.	SW
32	1400	At T-junction turn right towards le Bourg de Lestre		W
33	200	Arrive at the crossroads in the centre of le Bourg de Lestre		

Saint-Vaast-la-Hougue to le Bourg de Lestre 11.9km

Accommodation Note: No accommodation in Le Bourg, but option in QUINEVILLE, just 1,9km along the D421	Price	Opening	Animals
Machu Herlem Joëlle, 1 av Plage 50310 QUINEVILLE Tel: 0033 (0)2 33 21 40 30	B2	All Year	🐴
Camping	Price	Opening	Animals
Camping Municipal, 10 rue Port Sinope 50310 QUINEVILLE Tel: 0033 (0)2 33 21 07 38	B1	All Year	

Useful Contacts

Tourist Offices

17, av. de la Plage, 50310 QUINEVILLE Tel: 0033 (0)2 33 21 40 29
www.tourisme.fr/tourist-office/quineville.htm

Farrier

Bisson Christophe, port Filiolet 50360 PICAUVILLE Tel: 0033 (0)2 33 21 04 66

You are travelling along the **Cotentin Peninsula**, also known as the Cherbourg Peninsula. It is part of the Armorican Massif and lies between the estuary of the Vire River and Mont Saint Michel Bay. Divided into three areas: the headland of La Hague, the Cotentin Pass, and the valley of the Saire River (Val-de-Saire), the peninsula forms the bulk of the Manche département. Along with agriculture, the region is also famous for its shellfish and alcoholic beverages such as cider and calvados, made from local grown apples and pears. Due to its comparative isolation, the peninsula is one of the remaining strongholds of the Norman language, and the local dialect is known as Cotentinais.

Route Summary: another gentle section with only limited climbing. The section generally follows pathways and very minor roads. Some of the paths can be muddy or have deep grass, cyclists may wish to avoid these parts.

Way Point	Distance	Directions	Verification Point	Compass
1		From the crossroads in the centre of le Bourg de Lestre take the D421 in the direction of Lestre		SW
2	70	On the edge of the village bear left	Sign la Devise and the Salle Communale	W
3	50	Left turn in the direction of the Salle Communale		SW
4	150	After the road bends into a yard, keep straight ahead on the grassy track		SW
5	300	At the end of the track turn left onto a minor road		S
6	90	Turn left and cross the river by the footbridge. **Note:-** horses can ford the river if the conditions allow	La Sinope	SE
7	60	On the far side of the river take the track to the left		SE
8	300	At the top of the hill turn right onto a minor road	Briefly rejoin GR223	SW
9	60	At the next road junction take the right fork and climb the hill.		SW
10	550	After the road bends to the left go straight ahead passing a large house	Sign "Chemin des Landes"	E
11	350	At the T-junction turn right	GR223	S
12	200	At the crossroads turn left on the main road	D42	E
13	200	Take a right along a small road, rue de Bas Launay	Sign for the Chemin du Mont St Michel.	SE
14	500	The road becomes a track, bear left	Sign for the Village de Launay	S
15	190	Bear right on the track		S
16	1000	Keep straight on towards the farm	le Bas de Fontenay	S
17	150	At the T-Junction turn right on a minor road	Farm straight ahead	SW
18	300	At the T-junction turn right		NW

le Bourg de Lestre to Montebourg 10.8km

Way Point	Distance	Directions	Verification Point	Compass
19	60	Turn left into l'Avenue de Courcy	Château de Courcy and church on the left	SW
20	800	At T-junction turn right	Rue de Fontenay (D14)	NW
21	300	After the sign for the exit from Fontenay sur Mer, bear left on a grassy track		NW
22	500	The grass track comes out onto a very minor road turn right and immediately left		NW
23	160	At the junction in the Village d'Eglise, take the left fork heading for Vaudival on the D315	In the centre of the village pass the Church of St Basile	W
24	170	On the crown of the bend, turn right off the road and onto a grassy track, beside la Saussaie. **Note**:- to avoid potentially muddy ground, cyclists are advised to remain on the D315, turn right in Vaudival and follow the D71 into Montebourg	Leaving the GR223	W
25	300	Turn right over a footbridge and keep along the track		W
26	1200	At a T-junction in the track turn right		W
27	700	At crossroads, D63, take the track straight ahead	Farmhouse – le Decloncherie – to the left	SW
28	400	Keep to the track as it curves sharply around a double bend		SW
29	800	Bear right down the hill on the main track		W
30	180	Turn sharp left between a derelict house and a wall	Entering Montebourg	SW
31	180	At the T-junction with the main road turn left	D42	S
32	300	Turn right on rue Paul Lecacheux		NW
33	200	Arrive in the centre of Montebourg at the tourist office, adjacent to the Mairie	Rue du 11 Novembre.	

le Bourg de Lestre to Montebourg 10.8km

Accommodation	Price	Opening	Animals
Hôtel du Midi, 6 pl Albert Pelerin 50310 MONTEBOURG Tel: 0033 (0)2 33 41 22 16	B2	All Year	🐾

Equestrian Centre,

Les Ecuries de la Gare, La Cavée 50310 SAINT MARTIN D'AUDOUVILLE
Tel: 0033 (0)2 33 41 11 21 **Note**: 3.08 km from Montebourg

Useful Contacts

Tourist Offices

MONTEBOURG TOURIST OFFICE, 20, rue du Général Leclerc 50310 MONTEBOURG
Tel: 0033 (0)2 33 41 15 73
office.intercommunal-tourisme@wanadoo.fr   www.montebourg-tourisme-office.new.fr

Farrier

Valognes Michel, 1 rte Chêne 50360 BONNEVILLE (LA) Tel: 0033 (0)2 33 40 22 71

Montebourg was founded by William of Normandy in 1082, completely destroyed in 1792 and rebuilt on same site in 1892. Montebourg is the most significant St James site on the Cotentin peninsula. The Benedictine abbey had a chapel of St James and from the 12th to 17th century monks offered hospitality to travellers, including pilgrims from England. A Confrerie of St James has existed in Montebourg since at least 1690 and the crowning ceremony of St James has been enacted since 1281. Originally celebrated on the eve of the Feast of St James, though now usually on the nearest Saturday, a boy (a first communicant, named James) climbs a ladder to the statue of St James on the west front of the church, crowns it with a circlet of red flowers and places a bunch of red flowers in its hand. The church has two statues of St James, one on the west front and the other, an English alabaster depiction of St James as a pilgrim inside. Stained glass, installed in the 1960s, includes scenes from life of St James.

le Bourg de Lestre to Montebourg 10.8km

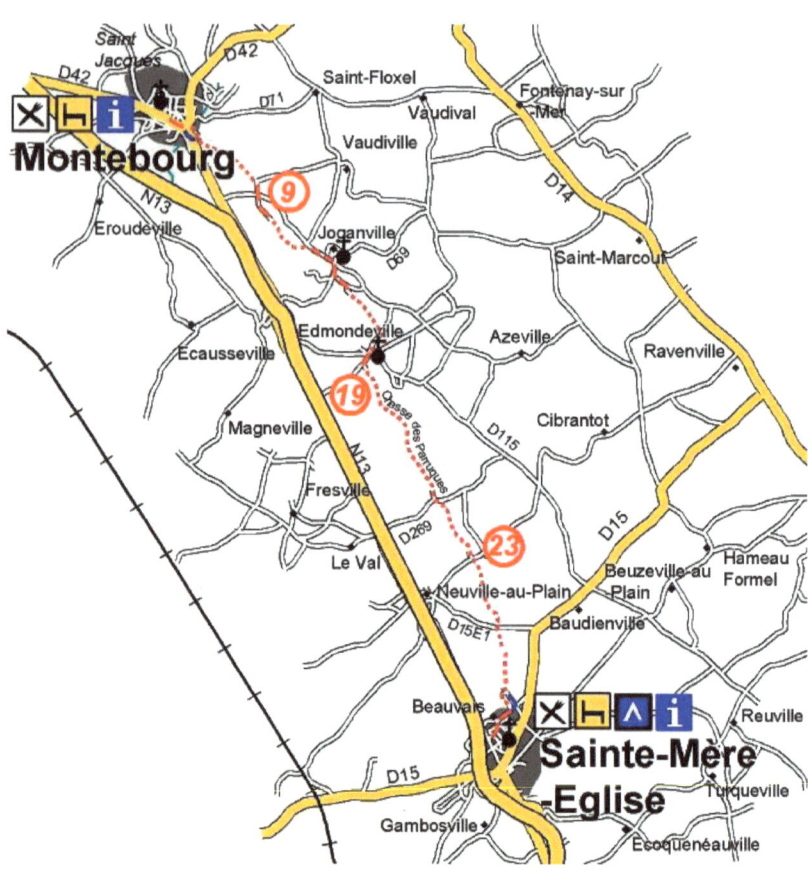

Montebourg to Sainte-Mère-Eglise 11.4km

Route Summary: an easy section for all groups on good tracks well separated from traffic.

Way Point	Distance	Directions	Verification Point	Compass
1		Leaving the entrance to the tourist office, turn left to descend the hill on rue Paul Lecacheux		SE
2	200	At the crossroads with the D42, turn left. **Note:**- horse riders should remain on the rue Paul Lecacheux for 200 metres and shortly after crossing river turn left to rejoin the GR223 at Way Point #5		NE
3	40	Turn right into narrow alley-way	Le Chemin de St Michel sign	SE
4	110	Straight ahead beside the traditional laverie		S

Way Point	Distance	Directions	Verification Point	Compass
5	120	At the end of the road follow the dogleg ending in a sharp left turn. **Note**:- horse-riders rejoin from the right		E
6	30	Turn right onto a grass track	Wooden Chemin du Mont St Michel sign	E
7	500	At a T-junction take the left to follow the Chasse de Jérusalem	Chemin du Mont St Michel sign	SE
8	500	At junction with a minor tarmac road take the right turn		S
9	200	At a crossroads go straight ahead	Large Chemin du Mont St Michel sign	SE
10	400	Just after a group of houses the road turns into a grassy track, go straight ahead	Joret	SE
11	400	As you pass the farm of Auberville keep straight ahead on the track		E
12	300	The track takes you back onto a minor road, turn right		SE
13	400	At the crossroads on the D115 in the village of Joganville, turn right	Pass the church	S
14	70	Take the left fork in the village centre	Beside Mairie	SE
15	300	Take the right fork between a house and a barn	Picard	SE
16	800	At the crossroads follow the track straight ahead		S
17	190	The track brings you to a minor road, turn right	Enter the village of Emondeville	SW
18	160	Turn right and left around the church	Follow D214 over crossroads	SW
19	200	Turn left down a track	Opposite a small group of houses, GR223	SE
20	1400	The track rejoins a minor road, continue straight ahead along the Chasse des Perrugues		SE
21	800	After a long easy descent take the left fork over a small river bridge	Le Brocq	SE
22	100	Immediately after the bridge turn right on a small grassy track		SE
23	900	The track brings you onto a minor road, continue straight over the crossroads	Towards the farm of les Osmonts	S

Montebourg to Sainte-Mère-Eglise 11.4km

Way Point	Distance	Directions	Verification Point	Compass
24	500	The track narrows into a grassy track. Continue straight on		S
25	500	Track emerges at a crossroads with a minor road, continue straight ahead along a gravelled path	Chasse du Monet	S
26	800	The track leads you into a forked road. Take the right fork around the house. **Note**:- there is a kissing gate ahead, riders should take the left fork and follow the road for 300 metres, turn right in the direction of Beauvais and rejoin the main route at Way Point #28		S
27	300	The track leads through a kissing gate between large farms and onto a private road, bear right	Michelle Boulevard	SE
28	100	On a minor road in between a number of houses, turn right		SW
29	180	Continue straight ahead	Rue de Beauvais	SW
30	100	At the junction in the middle of the village of Beauvais, take the left fork	Rue de Beauvais	SW
31	300	At T-junction turn left direction Centre Ville, Sainte-Mère-Eglise	Chemin du Mont St Michel sign	SE
32	500	Arrive in Sainte-Mère-Eglise at the Place du 6 Juin	Church to the left	

Montebourg to Sainte-Mère-Eglise 11.4km

Sainte-Mère-Eglise was made famous by the paratrooper John Steel and by the film "The Longest Day". John Steel managed to land on the church and his chute caught on the steeple. He hung there for two hours before being cut down by the Germans, taken prisoner and later released by the Americans. An effigy of John Steel is usually to be seen on the church. Inside the church there are two stained glass windows, one shows the Virgin Mary surrounded by paratroopers, the other shows St. Michael (patron saint of the paratroopers) and was dedicated in 1972. The liberation monument in the square was covered by a chute during the making of The Longest Day as the town mayor would not allow its removal. The Airborne Museum began in 1961 and houses many interesting artifacts including a DC3 aircraft used on D-day together with a glider. Outside the Town Hall is a pink marker stone of "Kilometre Zero". These markers were placed by the French Government in 1946, each Kilometre along the route taken by General Leclerc's Free French 2nd division, they can be seen from North Africa to the town of Bastogne the last town in Europe to be liberated. The town war memorial is situated behind the marker and plaques commemorate the liberation of the town.

Accommodation	Price	Opening	Animals
Ferme Riou, rue Ferme Riou 50480 SAINTE MÈRE EGLISE Tel: 0033 (0)2 33 41 63 40 fermederiou@hotmail.fr www.fermederiou.com	B2	All Year	🐴
Charlyne et Christian, 15 place du 6 Juin 50480 SAINTE MERE EGLISE Tel: 0033 (0)233215217 Mobile: 0033 (0)6 81 66 39 78 charlyne.berot@wanadoo.fr	B2	All Year	🐴
Ferme Manoir de la Fière 50480 SAINTE MERE EGLISE Tel: 0033 (0)2 33 41 31 77 poisson.yves2@wanadoo.fr	B2	All Year	🐴
Ferme Auberge de la Huberdiere, Le Pommier 50480 LIESVILLE SUR DOUVE Tel: 0033 (0)2 33 71 01 60 **Note**: slightly off the main route, direction Houesville, but a good possibility for horses		All Year	🐴

Camping	Price	Opening	Animals
CAMPING MUNICIPAL, rue du 505eme Airborne 50480 SAINTE MERE EGLISE Tel: 0033 (0)2 33 41 35 22	B1	All Year	🐴

Equestrian Centre,
Ecurie Gaumain, Village de l'Eglise 50480 BEUZEVILLE AU PLAIN
Mobile: 0033 (0)6 14 40 39 23 **Note**: 3.48km from St Mére Eglise

Useful Contacts
Tourist Offices
The Tourist Office of the District Communities of Sainte-Mère-Eglise - 6, rue Eisenhower 50480 SAINTE-MERE-EGLISE   Tel/ 0033 (0)2 33 21 00 33

Doctor
Renaud Erick, 27 r Verdun 50480 SAINTE MERE EGLISE Tel: 0033 (0)2 33 41 31 91

Veterinary
Simon De Picciotto Chauvet, 12 r Cap de Laine 50480 SAINTE MERE EGLISE
Tel: 0033 (0)2 33 21 01 31

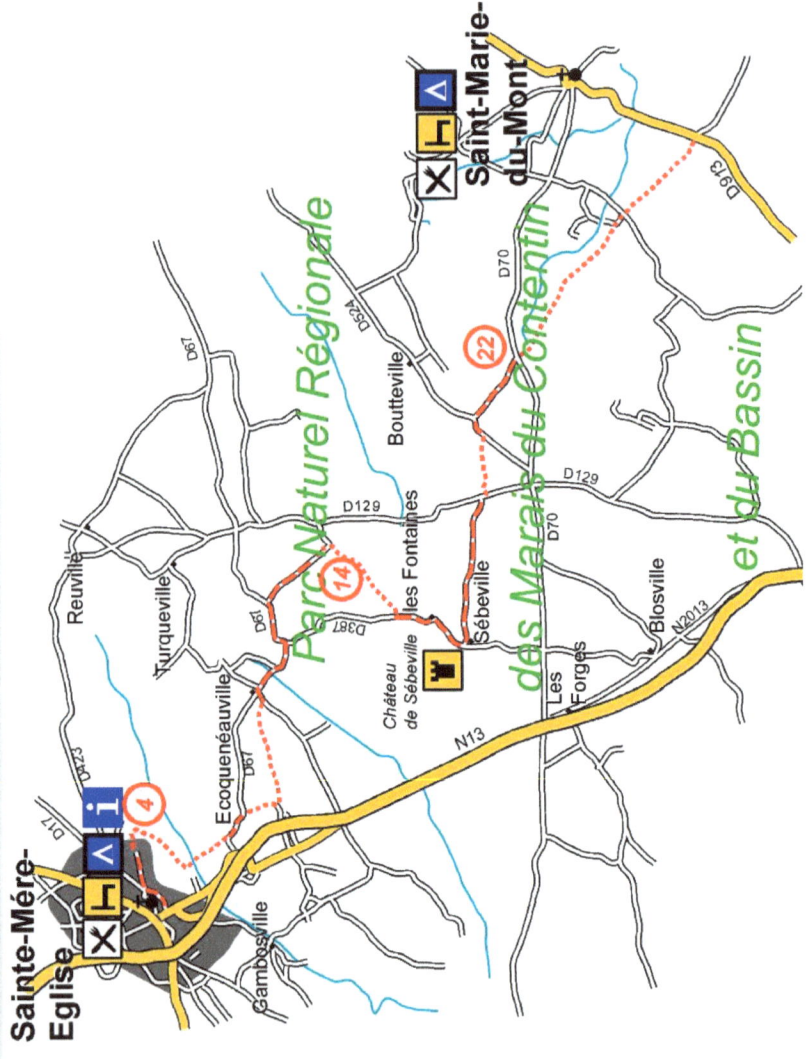

Route Summary: another easy section on broad farm tracks and minor roads. The end of the section falls 1 kilometre from the centre of Saint Marie du Mont where you can choose to continue on the next section or take the unfortunately busy road to the centre of the town.

Sainte-Marie-du-Mont, a small village, is best known for being the scene of military engagement between the American 101st Airborne Division and the German Wehrmacht on D-Day, June 6, 1944.

Way Point	Distance	Directions	Verification Point	Compass
1		From the junction of rue du Général de Gaulle and rue Eisenhower on the Place du 6 Juin, turn left to take rue Eisenhower	Church to the left	NE
2	190	Pass between the church and the Airborne Museum and continue towards Beuzeville on the D17		N
3	90	Turn right towards the camping and sports ground	Rue du 505 Airborne	E
4	500	The road changes into a gravel track, turn sharp right after passing camping ground	Camping ground to the right	SW
5	600	Take the left fork		SE
6	400	The track brings you onto a minor road bear left	D67	SE
7	200	Take the track to the right	Beside la Tournerie	S
8	300	Continue ahead on the track. Avoid the turning into Fauville		S
9	60	Turn left onto a grassy track		E
10	900	The track joins a minor road turn left at the T-junction		NE
11	70	At the T-junction with the D67 turn right into the village of Ecoquenéauville		E
12	70	Continue straight ahead on the D67	Pass beside the church	E
13	700	After le Grand Hameau turn right onto a gravelled road		SE
14	700	The road peters out into a track. At a crossroads in the track, turn right		SW
15	800	At a T-junction with a minor road(D387), turn left	House number 10 ahead	SW
16	600	Straight ahead through the hamlet of les Fontaines	Pass beside the château de Sébeville	S
17	80	After the château turn left on the road between a group of houses		E
18	1300	At T-junction, turn right	D129	SE
19	40	Turn left down a stony track		E

Sainte-Mère-Eglise to Sainte-Marie-du-Mont 11.2km

Way Point	Distance	Directions	Verification Point	Compass
20	500	The track brings you onto a minor road turn left	Towards Boutteville	NE
21	130	Just before the village, turn right in the direction of Sainte-Mairie-du-Mont	D524e	SE
22	600	At crossroads with a major road leading to Sainte-Marie-du-Mont and Utah Beach, go straight ahead on a small track	Chemin du Mont St Michel	SE
23	150	Continue straight ahead along a dirt track	Pass the farm of St. Martin on the left	SE
24	1000	At a T-junction of tracks bear left		SE
25	200	The track emerges onto a minor road bear right	Farm of Holdy to the left	SE
26	80	Leave road to continue straight ahead along a grassy track		SE
27	900	Crossroads where you can either turn left onto a main road (D913) and proceed to Sainte-Marie-de-Mont (1km). Or, continues straight ahead in the direction of Brucheville.	Church of Sainte-Marie-du-Mont visible on the hill-top to the left	

Accommodation	Price	Opening	Animals
Le Grand Hard, La Rivière 50480 SAINTE-MARIE-DU-MONT Tel: 0033 (0)2 33 71 25 74	B3	All Year	
M.Cornil, 38 place de l'Eglise 50480 SAINTE-MARIE-DU-MONT Tel: 0033 (0)2 33 71 91 06 Phil.cornil@free.fr www.lamaisondeshotes.com	B2	All Year	

Camping	Price	Opening	Animals
Camping Utah Beach, La Madeleine 50480 SAINTE-MARIE-DU-MONT Tel: 0033 (0)2 33 71 53 69 contact@camping-utahbeach.com www.camping-utahbeach.com/	B1	01 Avril - 30 Sept	
La Baie des Veys, Le Grand Vey 50480 SAINTE MARIE DU MONT Tel : 0033 (0)2 33 71 56 90 jerome.etasse@wanadoo.fr www.campinglabaiedesveys.com	B1	01 Avril - 30 Sept	

Sainte-Mère-Eglise to Sainte-Marie-du-Mont 11.2km

Carentan is a port on the Douve River at the base of the Cotentin Peninsula. The city is dominated by high ground to the southwest and southeast, all of which was under German control during WWII. The Germans flooded much of the Douve River floodplain prior to the invasion, resulting in impassable marshland, a tactic once used by Napoleon Bonaparte at the same location. Carentan has preserved an architectural heritage whose wealth and diversity is surprising. The Town Hall features a large square lined with 15th century arches. while Notre-Dame church and its organ are both listed monuments. Inside the church there are several representations of St Michael and a 15th century stained glass depicting St James. South side: the Holy family with St James as a boy with a pilgrim staff. North side: St James as a pilgrim.

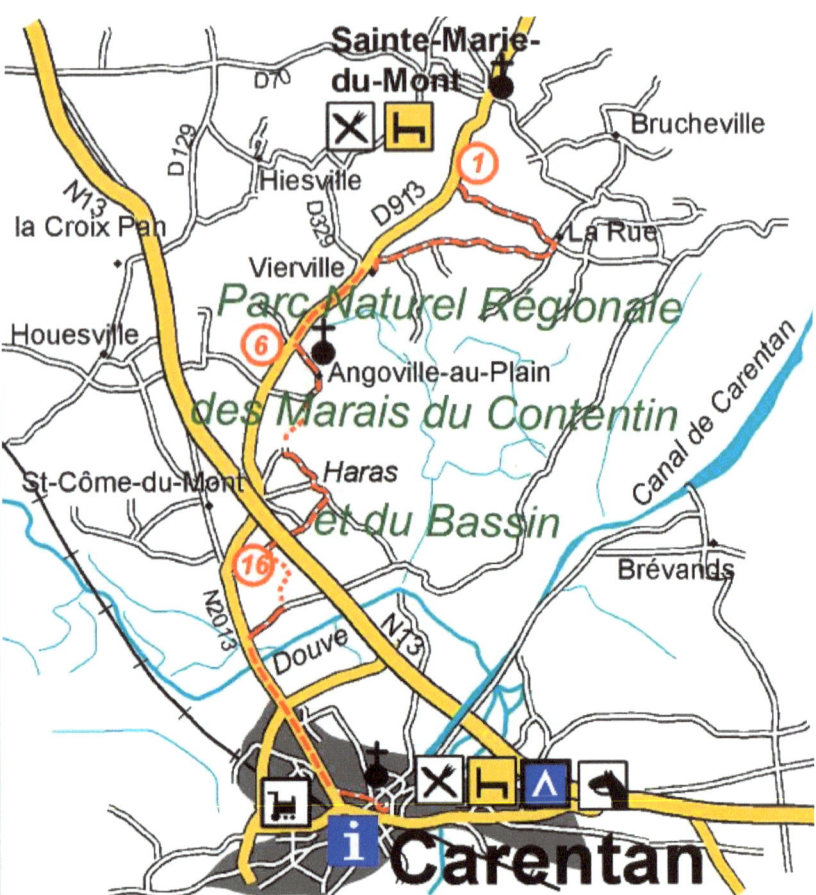

Route Summary: the route weaves on farm tracks and minor roads in an endeavour to avoid the busiest roads, but briefly rejoins the D913 and again encounters busy roads on the entry to the market town of Carentan.

Look out For: Vierville, late 16th c statue of St James with shell on hat.
Angoville-au-Plain, scallop shell and carved capital

Way Point	Distance	Directions	Verification Point	Compass
1		From the junction on the D913, 1 kilometre to the south-west of Sainte-Marie-du-Mont, take the road in the direction of Bruceville	D424E1	SE
2	1600	Turn right at the crossroads	Village of la Rue	SW
3	140	Take the right fork	D329	W
4	2300	Take the left fork into Vierville	Pass to the rear of church	SW

Way Point	Distance	Directions	Verification Point	Compass
5	300	At the T-junction with the main road (D913), take the left turn towards Carentan. **Caution:-** this is a very busy road		SW
6	1200	Turn left to Angoville-au-Plain		SE
7	500	In the village remain on the road passing in front of the memorial to two American medics	Church and memorial on the left	SW
8	300	Bear left towards the hamlet of les Préles	Pass a chambre d'hôtes	S
9	170	The road forks into two tracks, take the left fork	Farm buildings to the right	SW
10	500	The track emerges onto a minor road, turn left		SE
11	200	In the hamlet of la Haute Addeville the road forks, take the left fork		SE
12	300	At the T-junction turn left	Towards the stud, Haras, of Tamerville	E
13	140	Bear right and remain on the road passing the Haras		SE
14	160	The road forks, take right fork	La Basse Addeville	SW
15	400	At crossroads continue straight ahead under the N13	Pass château to the left, rejoin GR223	SW
16	500	Opposite the large farm (le Mont) leave the road and take the track to the left	Signpost to Les Ponts Douve	S
17	800	At a T-junction with a minor road take the right turn		SW
18	500	At the T-junction with main road (facing Espace Découverte) turn left and follow the Voie de Liberté	Signpost for Notre Dame de Carentan	SE
19	900	Continue straight ahead at the roundabout		SE
20	300	Remain on the D913 (Route de St Côme, rue de la 101éme Airborne)		SE
21	800	At fork in the road bear left	Rue Sébline	E
22	500	Arrive in the Market square in the centre of Carentan	La Poste to the left	

Sainte-Marie-du-Mont to Carentan 12.5km

Sainte-Marie-du-Mont to Carentan 12.5km

Accommodation	Price	Opening	Animals
26 rue 101 eme Airborne CARENTAN 50500 Tel: 0033 (0)2 33 71 00 43 chambres.carentan@bnb-normandie.com www.bnb-normandie.com	B3	All Year	🐴
L'Escapade, 34, rue de la Gare 50500 CARENTAN Tel : 0033 (0)2 33 42 02 00	B2	April - Sept	🐴
Le Vauban, 7, rue Sébline 50500 CARENTAN Tel : 0033 (0)2 33 71 00 20	B2	All Year	🐴
Camping	**Price**	**Opening**	**Animals**
Le Haut Dick, 30 chemin du Grand-Bas Pays 50500 CARENTAN Tel: 0033 (0)2 33 42 16 89 lehautdick@aol.com www.camping-municipal.com	B1	15/01/07 - 31/10/07	🐴

Equestrian Centre

Hinard Alain, 27 r Eglise 50500 AUVERS Tel/ 0033 (0)2 33 42 04 35 **Note:** 5.8km from Carentan

Useful Contacts
Tourist Offices

Office de Tourisme, bd Verdun 50500 CARENTAN   Tel: 0033 (0)2 33 71 23 50
info@ot-carentan.fr   www.ot-carentan.fr/

Doctor

Le Bart de la Broise Pierre, 8 pl Grand Valnoble 50500 CARENTAN
Tetl: 0033 (0)2 33 71 05 94

Veterinary

Clinique Vétérinaires Bisson-Cornière-Lemenil-Pasternak, 27 r 101ème Airborne 50500 CARENTAN   Tel: 0033 (0)2 33 42 13 09

Farrier

Avenel Christian,
23 r Gén Maxwell Taylor 50500 CARENTAN   Tel: 0033 (0)2 33 42 01 65

Accommodation	Price	Opening	Animals
Mme LAMBERTON Odile, 2 villages des Poissons 50500 SAINTENY Tel: 0033 (0)2 33 42 17 0 Mobile: 0033 (0)6 98 64 77 52	B2	All Year	

Equestrian Centre

Ecuries de la Minostrande, 28 r Minostrande 50190 MARCHESIEUX
Tel: 0033 (0)2 33 45 50 34 **Note**: 5.95 km from Sainteny

Carentan to Sainteny 11.9km

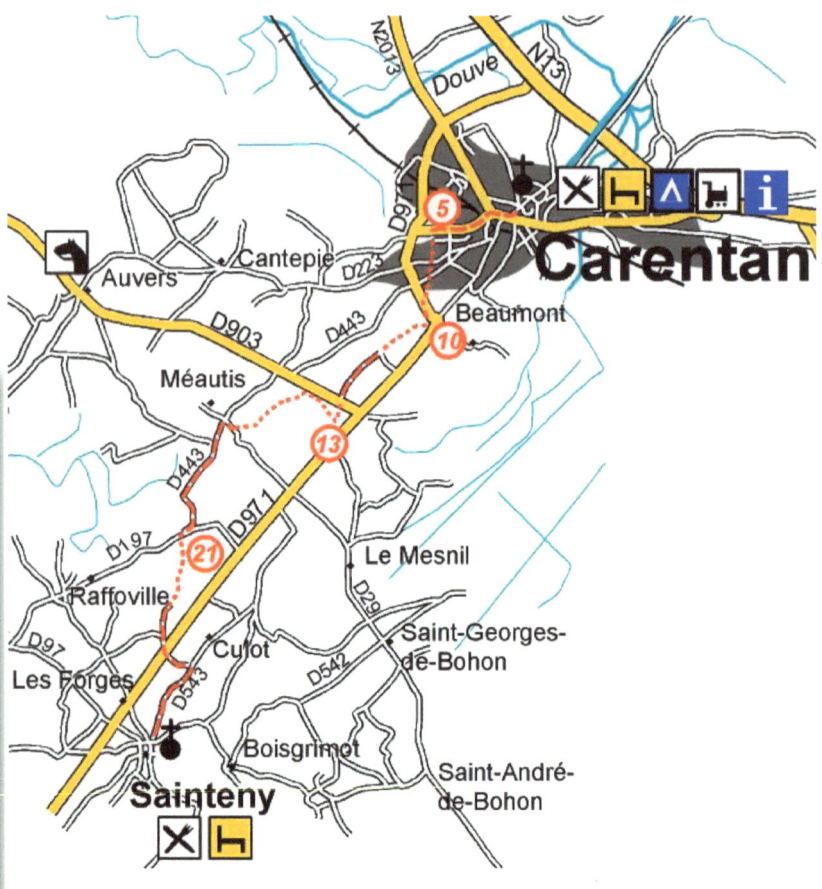

Carentan to Sainteny 11.9km

Route Summary: another generally easy flat section for all groups with only brief contact with the main roads.

Way Point	Distance	Directions	Verification Point	Compass
1		From the Place de la République take rue Holgate	Towards the railway station	SW
2	200	At the end of rue Holgate take a right turn in the direction of Valognes	Facing railway station	NW
3	200	At the traffic lights, turn left in the direction of Barneville and Carteret		SW
4	160	After crossing the railway bridge continue on the main road towards Périers		W

Way Point	Distance	Directions	Verification Point	Compass
5	700	Just as you leave the town limits turn left on a grassy path	Beside Carentan town sign	S
6	400	At crossroads with the D223, cross straight over		S
7	200	The track brings you onto the D443, turn right		SW
8	30	Cross the road and take an immediate left fork on a grassy track	Beside white gates	S
9	400	Emerge onto a busy main road turn left towards Périers	D971	SE
10	300	At the roundabout take the first exit to the right, onto small track and then immediately bear left	Beside farm buildings – le Bras Pendu	SW
11	900	At junction with a minor road, keep to the right towards a white house	la Chasse Verte	SW
12	900	The minor road meets a more major road (D903) which you cross straight over onto a grassy track		S
13	300	Turn sharp right		NW
14	600	The track comes to a fork beside a farm, bear left		W
15	80	Immediately after the farm, turn left in front of the house		SW
16	700	Keep straight ahead, avoiding the turn-off		W
17	300	The track leads onto a minor road, turn right in front of a stone cross in the direction of the school	Village of Méautis	NW
18	170	At the crossroads in Méautis, turn left on the D443		SW
19	400	Avoid the turning to Auvers (D543) and go straight on		S
20	1400	At a T-junction turn right on the D197	la Croix Picard	SW
21	80	Turn left up a grassy track		S
22	600	At a T-junction on the track, turn left		S
23	500	Avoid the driveway into the farm and bear left towards a smaller house	La Fresnene	S
24	400	At the fork, bear left	Towards le Sablonnet	S
25	300	Emerge at a crossroads with the D971. Continue on the track ahead	Towards Ventigny	SE
26	400	At a T-junction with the D543, turn right		SW
27	1300	Arrive in the centre of Sainteny	Church to the left	

Carentan to Sainteny 11.9km

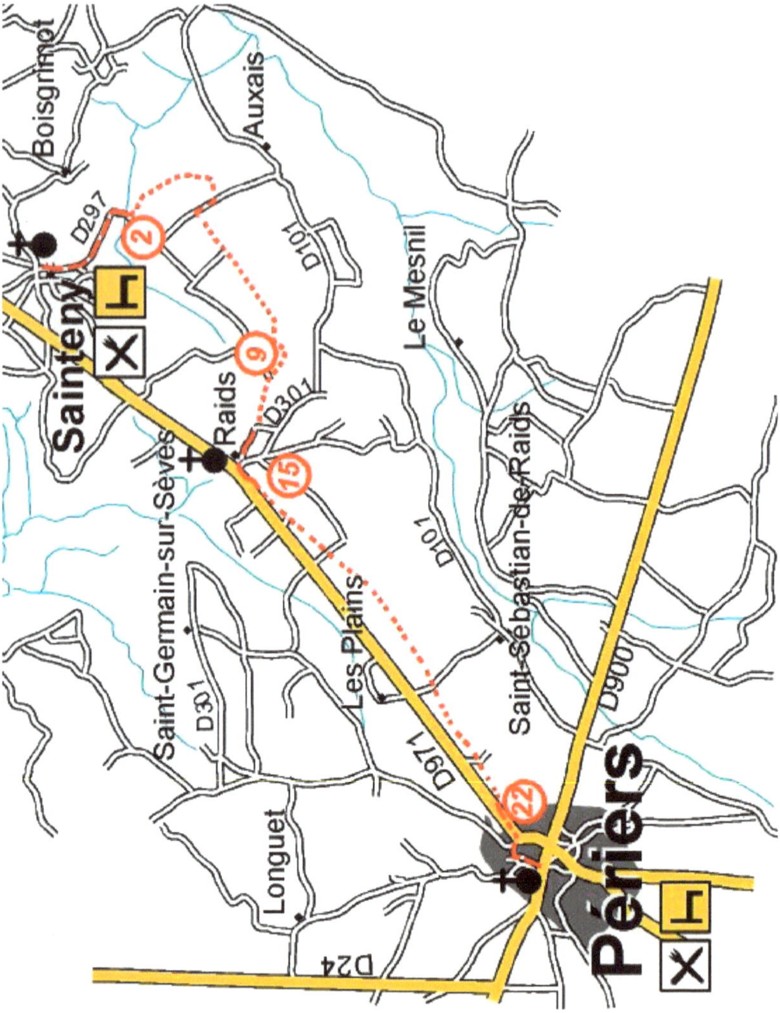

Saintenay to Périers 12.6km

Route Summary: the route continues on level ground over farm tracks and minor roads until reaching the village of Raids. After Raids, the path running parallel to the main road can be difficult with tall grass and muddy conditions.

Way Point	Distance	Directions	Verification Point	Compass
1		At the crossroads, in the village of Sainteny, go left towards Auxais on the D297	Pass beside the Mairie	SE
2	1500	Continue on the D297 until reaching the bottom of the hill, turn left onto a dirt track	Sign Chemin de St Michel	SE
3	600	Pass beside the farm gates and go straight ahead on the grassy track		S
4	400	At a crossroads of tracks, turn right	Sign Chemin de St Michel	W
5	300	At T-junction with D297, turn right		NW
6	300	Turn left down a grassy track	Château on the right before you turn	SW
7	600	At crossroads in the tracks go straight ahead		SW
8	1200	Keep to the main grassy track	There is a series of bends and a kissing gate	W
9	700	At a junction of tracks continue straight ahead on the grassy track		NW
10	400	The track bends and emerges into a slightly broader track. Keep straight ahead on this track		W
11	200	At a junction with a number of paths go straight ahead onto a tarmac road	Grey house, Croix Regnault	NW
12	400	Enter the village of Raids and join the D301. Go straight ahead towards the main road	Pass church on the right	W
13	110	At the T-junction with the main road (D971), turn left in the direction of Périers. Keep to the pavement on the left side of the road		SW
14	80	Almost immediately bear left onto a very narrow grassy track running at a shallow angle to the main road. **Note:-** the track can be muddy with tall grass, cyclists may wish to remain on the D971 until the main route rejoins the road at Way Point #23, before entering Périers	The path will run parallel to the road until reaching the town of Périers	SW

Saintenay to Périers 12.6km

Way Point	Distance	Directions	Verification Point	Compass
15	300	Keep straight ahead on the track as you pass beside a house and cross the driveway	Parallel to the main road	SW
16	1000	The grassy track comes out onto a minor road. Cross the road and continue on the grassy track	Kissing gates	SW
17	800	At an intersection with other tracks, straight ahead between the trees and parallel to the main road	After passing under the second high voltage line	SW
18	700	At a fork in the track follow the left fork, keeping parallel to the main road		SW
19	400	At crossroads with a minor road, cross straight over	Beside the farm, Maison Neuve	SW
20	400	At a crossroads of tracks go straight on	St Michel sign on a tree	SW
21	700	At a junction of tracks and a minor road, continue straight over the minor road	Remain parallel to the main road	SW
22	600	The track broadens and leads to a fork. Take the right fork towards the main road	Industrial buildings ahead	NW
23	60	At the T-junction with the main road turn left	Towards roundabout	SW
24	300	Enter Périers and turn right at the roundabout	Follow sign to Centre Ville	SW
25	500	Arrive in Périers centre, Place de Gaulle	Beside church	

Saintenay to Périers 12.6km

Accommodation	Price	Opening	Animals
Hotel de la Poste, avenue de la Gare, 50190 PÉRIERS Tel: 0033 (0)2 33 46 64 01	B2	All Year	

Useful Contacts

Doctor

Alexandre Luc, 7 r Gare 50190 PERIERS   Tel: 0033 (0)2 33 07 61 70

Veterinary

Kazandjian Avenel Grare, Christophe Ferreira, Le Mexique 50190 PERIERS
Tel: 0033 (0)2 33 46 63 01

Farriers

Hinard Serge, 1 r Vallée 50570 LOZON   Tel: 0033 (0)2 33 56 22 25

Periers - points of interest:
A monument commemorating the liberation of Périers by the soldiers of the 90th American Infantry Division under general Landrum. Inaugurated in 2000, this monument represents three 90th Division's soldiers killed in the area.
Periers is also a north/south and east/west crossing point for Roman roads.
In the market square, look out for a relic of the True Cross and the unusual hexagonal *lanterne des morts*.

Périers to Saint-Sauveur-Landelin 9.4km

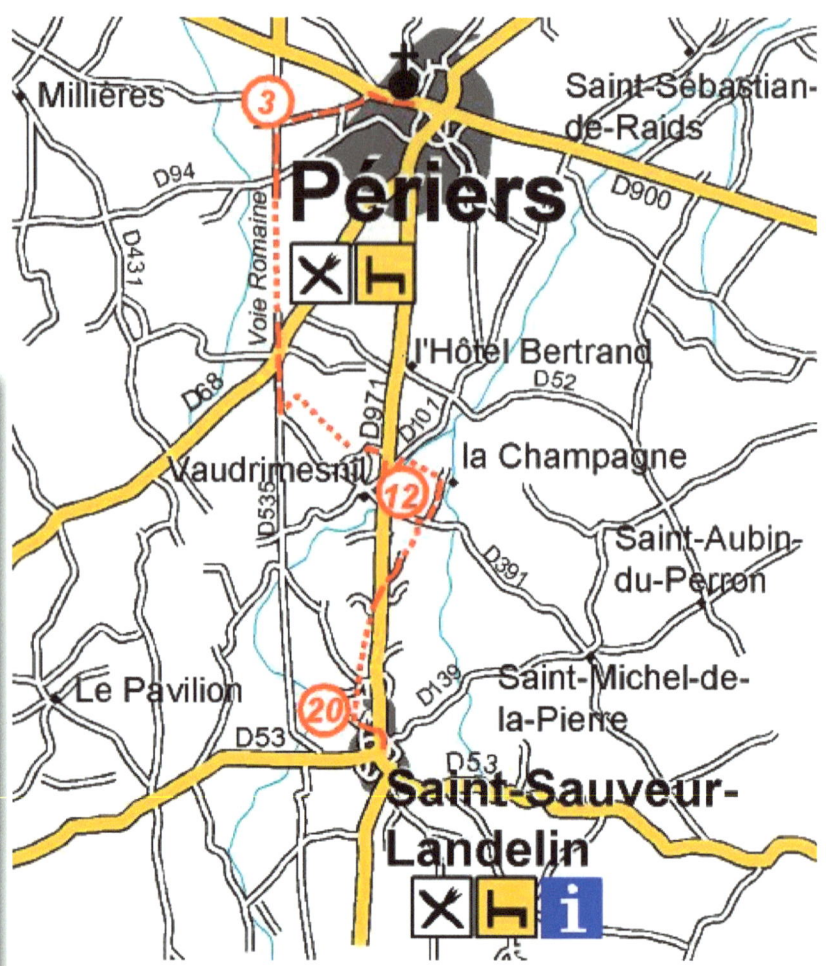

Route Summary: another easy section for all groups, caution is needed at each crossing of the busy D971.

Way Point	Distance	Directions	Verification Point	Compass
1		Starting from the magnificent gothic church of Périers, take the D900, in the direction of Lessay	Rue de Pont l'Abbé	W
2	400	Turn left	Rue du Clos Thorel.	W
3	1100	At the crossroads turn left	The long, straight Voie Romaine	S
4	2300	At the crossroads with the D68, cross straight over, direction Vaudrimesnil	Voie Romaine (D535)	S

Way Point	Distance	Directions	Verification Point	Compass
5	500	Turn sharp left down a grassy track do not take the fork on the minor road in the direction of Vaudrimesnil.	Beside a pond surrounding a crucifix	NE
6	200	Turn right		SE
7	800	At T-junction with a minor road, turn left	Beside la Blotterie	E
8	400	At T-junction with major road turn right	D971	S
9	150	Turn left on the D101 in the direction St Sébastien		NE
10	200	Turn right across footbridge with a wooden balustrade onto a grassy track	Just before the hamlet of le Réuté.	SE
11	300	Go straight across the disused railway track		SE
12	120	At T-junction turn right	House, la Champagne, directly in front	S
13	400	At the T-junction turn right	Under the old railway bridge	W
14	70	Just after railway bridge turn left, ignore "no entry"	Chemin de St Michel sign	SW
15	500	The track becomes a tarmac road continue straight ahead.		SW
16	200	Cross the D971 once again	Chemin de St Michel sign	SW
17	160	Leave the group of houses and go straight ahead on a grass track, again ignore the no entry sign	Le Pestils	S
18	800	The track brings you out onto a minor road bear slightly left		S
19	70	Go straight up the gravel track ignoring the no entry sign.		S
20	300	At crossroads with a minor road (D139e) turn left	Towards Saint-Sauveur-Lendelin	SE
21	300	At crossroads with D971 turn right into the centre of Saint-Sauveur-Lendelin		S
22	160	Arrive at the centre of Saint-Sauveur-Lendelin	Crossroads with D53	

Périers to Saint-Sauveur-Lendelin 9.4km

Accommodation	Price	Opening	Animals
Harmonie des Saisons, 2 r Mar Leclerc 50490 SAINT SAUVEUR LENDELIN Tel: 0033 (0)2 33 07 79 08	B2	All Year	

Useful Contacts
Tourist Offices
Office du Tourisme, 1 r 8 Mai 1945 50490 SAINT SAUVEUR LENDELIN
Tel: 0033 (0)2 33 19 19 24

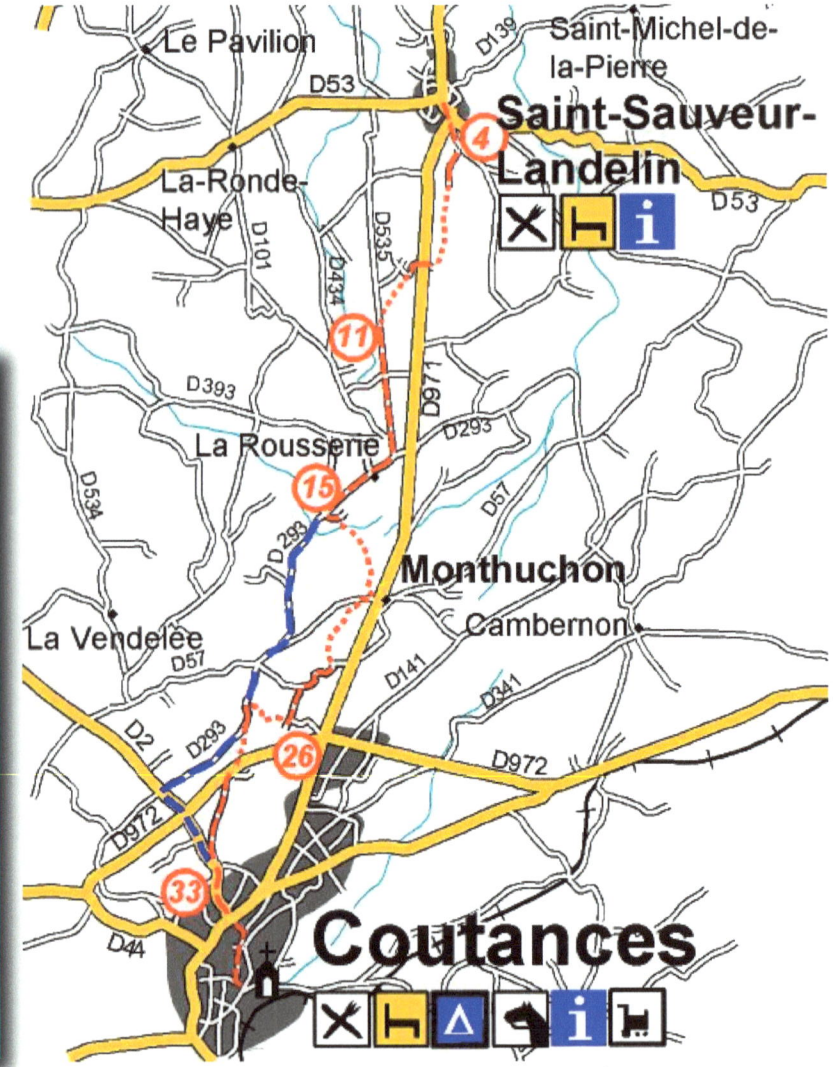

Route Summary: the route is largely off-road on farm tracks, but with some short steep climbs and some narrow sections. Horse and bike riders are recommended to take the road option for the approach to Coutances.

Look Out For: Monthuchon, Croix Burnel, 1635, erected in memory of an irish pilgrim, who having made a vow of silence, was murdered in Monthuchon on his return journey from St-Jacques.

Way Point	Distance	Directions	Verification Point	Compass
1		At the crossroads with the rue du Général Bradley (D971) and rue du 8 mai 1945 go straight ahead on the D971	Direction Coutances	S
2	170	Turn left at the traffic lights in the direction of St Lô	D53	SE
3	100	Turn right at the school	Rue de Rupalet	S
4	300	On leaving the town, turn right in the direction Le Haute Bourg - ignore the "no through road" sign		S
5	500	Continue straight ahead	Pass beside the Maison en Terre	S
6	190	The track forks, take the left fork		S
7	700	At the top of the hill there is a 3-way junction, take the right turn		W
8	110	The track meets a crossroads with the D971, cross over and follow road as it turns to the left	Signs for La Colerie and La Gabousserie	SW
9	170	Take the lane straight ahead passing beside the farm yard		SW
10	300	The path brings you to a group of houses, continue straight on down a dirt track	Farm gate and buildings, la Gabousserie, on your right	S
11	300	The track emerges at a junction with a minor road, bear left	D535	S
12	500	Continue straight ahead	Pass between la Forcherie and la Petite Perque	S
13	700	At the crossroads go straight ahead		S
14	200	At the bottom of the hill pass a group of houses and turn right at the T-junction	La Rousserie	SW
15	900	Turn left. **Note**:- Cyclists and horse-riders can avoid narrow tracks and steps by continuing on the D293, and entering Coutances on the D2 , rejoining the main route at Way Point #33	La Gluaiserie (Nos, 41 – 49)	SE
16	100	In front of the houses turn right on gravel path		SE
17	400	Continue straight on up a very narrow track		S
18	500	The path brings you up a steep climb to a group of houses, take the left fork towards the main road		SE

Saint-Sauveur-Landelin to Coutances 11.7km

Way Point	Distance	Directions	Verification Point	Compass
19	120	At the T-junction with the D57, turn right	Enter Monthuchon and pass by the Mairie	W
20	160	On descending the hill, take the road on the left		SW
21	20	Turn right onto a grass track	Before water tower	SW
22	800	At junction with a minor road bear right	Corrugated iron barn in front	SW
23	150	Continue straight ahead	Pass by la Michellière	W
24	90	Follow road as it bends to the left	GR223 joins from the right	SW
25	300	Take the left fork	Follow the sign for le Vaurecent	SW
26	300	At fork at the beginning of a group of houses, bear right	No Though Road.	SW
27	80	As you come to the drive into a house, take the unmade track to the right		NW
28	600	At T-junction with a minor road, turn left		S
29	200	As the road bends to the right, take unmade track to the left		S
30	200	The track comes down onto a minor road cross straight over and continue on the small path		SW
31	300	The track emerges onto a minor road, close by a major road, turn right	Pass under road bridge	S
32	70	Immediately after the bridge turn right and follow the GR223 to the south		S
33	1100	At the junction with the D2, turn left	Rue de l'Ecluse Chette	S
34	600	At the crossroads with the D971 go straight ahead and take rue du Maréchal Joffre leading to the rue St Nicolas and the Rue Tancréde.		S
35	500	Arrive in Coutances centre	The Cathedral of Notre Dame is to your left	

Saint-Sauveur-Landelin to Coutances 11.7km

Accommodation	Price	Opening	Animals
La Taverne du Parvis, Place du Parvis 50200 COUTANCES Tel: 0033 (0)2 33 45 13 55 www.lataverneduparvis.com	B2	All Year	🐴
Etap, 14, Allee du Chateau de la Mare 50200 COUTANCES Mobile : 0033 (0)8 92 68 40 19	B2	All Year	🐴
M. et Mme Grieu, 30 rue du Palais de Justice 50200 COUTANCES Tel: 0033 (0)2 33 45 12 42	B2	All Year	🐴

Camping	Price	Opening	Animals
Camping Les Vignettes, Route de Saint-Malo-de-la-Lande 50200 COUTANCES Tel: 0033 (0)2 33 45 43 13 servicesdessports@ville-coutances.fr	B1	All Year	🐴

Equestrian Centre,
Centre Equestre la Galaisière, La Galaisière 50200 SAINT PIERRE DE COUTANCES
Tel: 0033 (0)2 33 47 91 28   ph.maurice@hotmail.fr   **Note:** 1.6km from Coutances

Useful Contacts
Tourist Offices
Tourisme et Culture en Pays de Coutances, Place Georges Leclerc 50200 COUTANCES
Tel: 0033 (0)2 33 19 08 10   tourisme-coutances@wanadoo.fr
www.ville-coutances.fr

Doctor
Rodet Christian, 70 bd Alsace Lorraine 50200 COUTANCES
Tel: 0033 (0)2 33 45 37 24

Talbourdet Vincent, 34 quai Henri Chardon 50760 BARFLEUR
Tel: 0033 (0)2 33 43 24 00

Veterinary
Clinique Vétérinaire des Docteurs Blier Lepourry et Rouxel, 1 pl Gén Wood 50200 COUTANCES   Tel: 0033 (0)2 33 45 17 68

Farrier
La Forge de Courcy, 4 Les Fleuderies 50200 COURCY   Mobile: 0033 (0)6 70 58 29 59

Coutances is an attractive town teetering on a small hilltop and primarily interesting for its *Cathédrale de Notre Dame*. Essentially Gothic, it is still very Norman in its unconventional blending of architectural traditions. Also worth taking time out to visit: the Cathedral of St-Pierre, the church of St Nicolas and the Town hall, which incorporates the tower from St James' chapel. In addition, Coutances is well known for its jazz festival which takes over the town in early May and features European jazz. Well worth arranging your pilgrimage schedule in order to take a break here.

Route Summary: the section is initially off-road crossing low hills before descending into the coastal plain. For walkers there is the opportunity to pass close beside the estuary of la Sienne, while riders are advised to take to the roads to avoid numerous stiles.

Way Point	Distance	Directions	Verification Point	Compass
1		From the Cathedral cross the square – Parvis Notre Dame	Mairie on the left	W
2	110	Turn left	Rue Daniel	SW
3	60	Bear right and descend the hill on rue Quesnel-Canveaux	Jardin Public on the left	NW
4	190	At the traffic lights turn left		NW
5	50	Turn sharp right on the D44 rue de Saint Malo. **Note**:- Pedestrians can take the steps	Red and white GR sign, directly below local signs to the Parc des Sports etc	NW
6	90	Turn left down a small partly cobbled road	Rue des Piliers	NW
7	190	Take the second turning to the left	Chemin des Vignettes, GR223.	SW
8	80	Straight ahead on a gravel path	Between a house and a garage	S
9	50	Continue straight up the hill		S
10	50	Bear right and continue up the hill	Avoid the fork marked with a red and white cross	SW
11	160	At the top of hill turn left		SW
12	300	Beside the greenhouses bear left. Avoid the gravel path and continue on the tarmac		W
13	70	After passing the greenhouses on right, take unmade track to the right	Sign for the Biodiversity de la Bocage Normand	SW
14	110	Turn to the right and continue along the unmade track	You will enter a car park with some modern buildings straight ahead	NW
15	300	At fork bear left	Keep to the left-side of the water tower	W
16	200	Straight ahead	Under the large road bridge	W
17	300	At the fork in the gravelled track take the left fork		SW
18	600	Keep straight on past turnings on both sides	Hamlet of le Bois	SW
19	400	At the T-junction take the road to the left		S
20	500	At the crossroads with the D20 in the village of Bricqueville la Blouette go straight across	Rue du Val de Soulle	S
21	500	After village the road peters out into a track, continue straight ahead		SW

Coutances to Regnéville-sur-Mer 13.9km

Way Point	Distance	Directions	Verification Point	Compass
22	1400	Turn sharp right	After passing les Moulins	W
23	600	At the T-junction with a major road, turn left	D20	SW
24	300	Remain on the D20 through the village of le Pont de la Roque		SW
25	300	At the roundabout turn left		S
26	300	Cross the bridge over la Sienne	Beside the ruined bridge	SW
27	190	Immediately after the bridge turn right onto the grass, and follow the red and white GR signs. **Note**:- The pathway follows the estuary, but unfortunately the area is used extensively for grazing sheep, as a result there are many difficult stiles. Riders should take the cycle track to the top of the hill and turn right onto the D156. For 6 kilometres, skirt the estuary on the D156 and D249, finally returning to the D156 to enter Regnéville-sur-Mer and rejoin the main route at the end of this section	Beside picnic area and the house le Mesnil	NW
28	2700	Follow the path along the estuary, remaining close by the hedgerow, until opposite the church of Heugueville sur Sienne. Turn left following the GR signs		SW
29	90	At the top of the hill turn right		W
30	1000	At the minor road T-junction, take the road to the right	Keep the estuary and sea to your right	SW
31	400	In the centre of the hamlet of le Prey, turn right	The route turns back towards the estuary and the sea	N
32	110	Pass through the metal wicket gate and turn left to follow the landward edge of the estuary around the headland		SW
33	2000	Turn right to leave the estuary track and join the D156		S
34	200	Arrive in Regnéville sur Mer at the junction of the D156 with rue de Vaudredoux	Beside auberge	

78

Accommodation	Price	Opening	Animals
Hostellerie de la Baie, LE PORT 50590 REGNEVILLE SUR MER Tel: 0033 (0)2 33 07 43 94	B2	All Year	
Mme Lallement Micheline, Village de la Rousserie 50590 REGNÉVILLE SUR MER Tel: 0033 (0)2 33 45 00 27	B2	All Year	

Equestrian Centre,

Bourdon Jean-François, 45 av Sports 50590 HAUTEVILLE SUR MER
Tel: 0033 (0)2 33 45 56 20 **Note:** 4.07km from Regnéville sur Mer

The **Château de Regnéville** is a ruined 14th century castle. Built at the edge of the Sienne river estuary, it was intended to protect the important dry harbour of Regnéville-sur-Mer, one of most active of the Cotentin Peninsula from the Middle Ages until the 17th century. Partly dismantled at the end of the Hundred Years' War, it was much altered during the 17th and 18th centuries. Today, archaeological excavations and restoration work are gradually bringing it back to life. The keep of Regnéville, with its characteristic silhouette, became the symbol of the town and its imposing mass dominates the remains of the castle. In spite of an antiquated architecture for the 14th century, the keep seems to have been well built. It adopted the square plan and corner buttresses so characteristic of Romanesque castlse and monuments (Caen, Falaise, Norwich). The restoration of the castle, undertaken in 1994, seeks to restore the appearance at the time of Roulland de Gourfaleur, at the end of the 16th century.

Useful Contacts

Tourist Offices

Regnéville-sur-Mer Tourist Information Office, 8, rue du Port 50590 REGNEVILLE-SUR-MER Tel: 0033 (0)2 33 45 88 71

Doctor

Ancelin François, 7 r Port 50590 REGNEVILLE SUR MER
Tel: 0033 (0)2 33 47 63 77

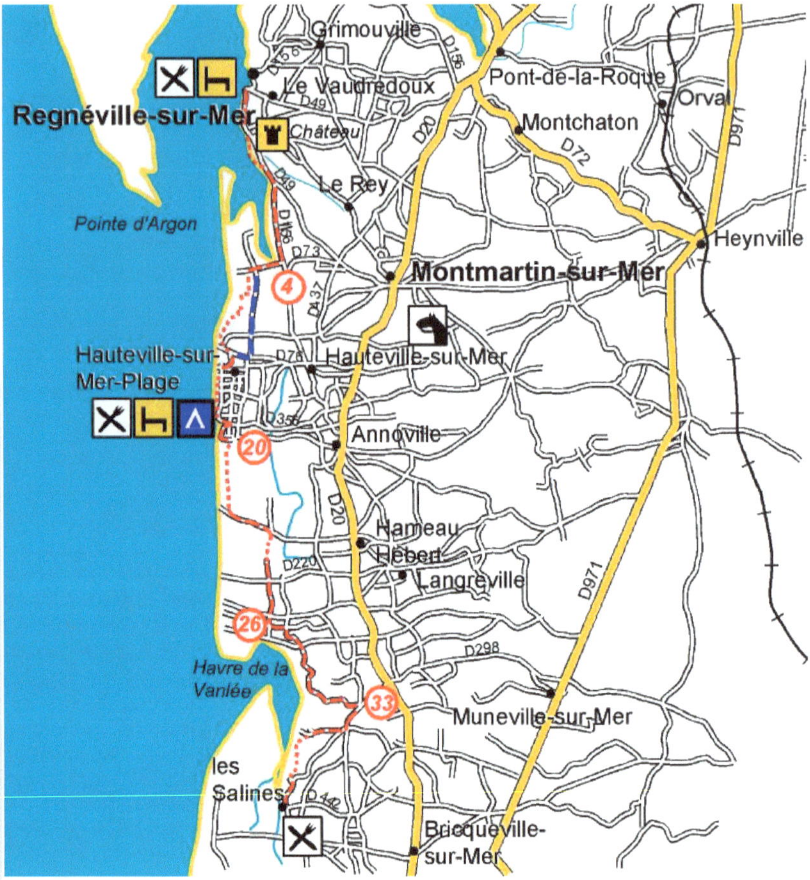

Regnéville sur Mer to les Salines 14.4km

Route Summary: the route proceeds south on pathways parallel to the beach, weaving through the seaside communities and caravan parks. Horse and bike riders need to follow the road on occasion to bypass a series of stiles.

Waymark	Distance	Directions	Verification Point	Compass
1		From the junction between the coast road and the D49 turn right along the coast road	Junction beside the Auberge	S
2	500	Leave the rue du Port and turn right into the car park. Ahead take the gravel path with the sea on the right	Beside l'Hostellerie de la Baie	SE
3	1000	Take the right fork onto the D156 in the direction of direction Hautville-sur-Mer	Shortly after passing the boatyard	S
4	1300	Turn right on the D73 and cross the Canal de Passerin		W
5	500	Walkers continue straight ahead. **Note:-** there are a number of stiles on the next series of paths. Horseback and bike riders should turnleft and follow the road keeping parallel to the sea-shore. Turn right at the T-junction to rejoin the main route at Waypoint #14		W
6	130	Just before reaching the sea, there is car park on left. Turn left and go straight ahead onto a grassy track	GR signs	S
7	200	Follow the track ahead and cross a wooden stile		S
8	170	At the next stile turn right		W
9	120	Cross stile and turn left	Beside a wire fence and the beach	S
10	180	After another stile turn right and immediately left	Continue parallel to the sea	S
11	190	After a series of stiles turn right in front of a caravan site		W
12	120	On reaching the beach turn left and walk along the beach		SW
13	400	At end of the tarmac track, turn left and proceed inland		SE
14	200	The road forks, take the right fork between houses and caravans. **Note:-** cyclists and riders rejoin from the road ahead	Rue des Garennes	S

Regnéville sur Mer to les Salines 14.4km

81

Waymark	Distance	Directions	Verification Point	Compass
15	300	At the T-junction turn right back towards the beach	Hauteville-sur-Mer-Plage	W
16	180	Facing the sea turn left on the path beside the beach. Note:- there is a parallel cycle track and restrictions on beach access for horse-riders. Horse-riders should investigate the cycle route or beach according to the posted restrictions and time of year		S
17	800	Turn left back into the town along the D356		E
18	100	Turn right, on rue de d'Annoville	Pass beside the gite d'etape	S
19	300	On reaching the sand dunes follow the track to the left and inland		E
20	130	Turn next right onto an unmade track, passing to the right-side of the group of trees	Sign Circuit de Dunes	S
21	1100	At the gate and car park, go straight on		S
22	110	At the end of the rough track return onto tarmac and take the left turn away from the sea		SE
23	700	At the crossroads turn right onto an unmade track between trees	Sign Circuit de Dunes	S
24	700	At the crossroads with the D220 go straight over on the unmade track	Chemin des Marais	S
25	500	At crossroads with a tarmac road, go straight over and keep on the sandy track		S
26	160	At a crossroads of sandy tracks with caravans all around take the left turn	Charriere Patin	E
27	300	At a T-junction of tracks take the track to the right	Chemin des Matelots	SE

Regnéville sur Mer to les Salines 14.4km

Waymark	Distance	Directions	Verification Point	Compass
28	300	Cross straight over the tarmac road and continue on the unmade road	Chemin des Matelots	S
29	500	At a fork in the tracks, take the right fork		S
30	50	Almost immediately turn right onto a small grass track	GR sign	SW
31	160	Continue along the top of the cliff on a sandy track		SE
32	200	Return to a tarmac road, D298, and follow it to the right	Rue de Ruet	E
33	600	At the junction of 5 roads, turn sharp right in the direction of les Salines	Rue des Salines	SW
34	400	At the next crossroads take a right on the D278 towards the sea		SW
35	150	Take the right fork and continue towards the sea		W
36	300	At the next junction take the left fork	Continue on the D278	W
37	160	Leave the road taking the track to the left		S
38	90	The track forks again take the right fork towards the sea		S
39	800	At the T-junction with a tarmac road turn right towards les Salines		S
40	300	Arrive in les Salines on the D442		

Regnéville sur Mer to les Salines 14.4km

Accommodation	Price	Opening	Animals
Mahe Lucien Chambres, rte 1, Mont Rabec 50290 BRICQUEVILLE SUR MER Tel: 0033 (0)2 33 51 71 79	B2	All Year	🐴

Camping	Price	Opening	Animals
Camping municipal les Garennes, 12 rue des Garennes 50590 HAUTEVILLE SUR MER Tel: 0033 (0)2 33 46 28 93	B1	01/04/08 - 01/11/08	🐴
Camping municipal du Sud, Avenue du sud 50590 HAUTEVILLE SUR MER Tel: 0033 (0)2 33 47 52 28 Mobile: 0033 (0)6 30 73 18 32	B1	15/06/08 - 15/09/08	🐴

Equestrian Centre
Bourdon Jean-François, Centre Equestre 45 av Sports 50590 HAUTEVILLE SUR MER Tel: 0033 (0)2 33 45 56 20

Useful Contacts
Tourist Offices
Office du Tourisme Syndicat d'Initiative, 10 av L'Aumesle 50590 HAUTEVILLE SUR MER Tel: 0033 (0)2 33 47 51 80

While travelling through Normandy, it is worth taking note of the local cuisine. As can be expected of a region boasting both an extensive coastline and a fertile interior, the range of produce on offer in Normandy is varied and rich, making Norman cooking one of the *grand cuisines* of France. The extensive coastline provides an abundance of fresh

seafood, the lush green pastures of the Normandy countryside makes ideal grazing for dairy herds and cattle and the apple orchards give delicious fruit that is used to make a variety of ciders and Calvados. It is therefore not surprising that Normandy cuisine has a distinct identity with its own favourite ingredients: apples, cider, cream and butter. Normandy is the largest producer of *huîtres creuses* in France - so much so that one in every three oysters consumed in France comes from Normandy. Some of the region's finest oysters come from St-Vaast-la-Hougue followed by the Bay of Mont St-Michel and the Isigny-Grandcamp coast. Equally popular are *coquilles St-Jacques* (scallops) that take pride of place in most coastal restaurants in the winter as scallop fishing is only allowed from October to May. Normandy is the number 1 region in France for scallop fishing, producing between 50 and 75% of the country's scallops. Lower Normandy, and in particular the department of La Manche, produces 25-30% of France's mussels. All of Normandy's mussel producers market the mussels under the collective national brand Moules de Bouchot, which was registered in 1994 and guarantees a method of culture that will produce high-quality mussels. Dairy products are also a serious business throughout Normandy and butter is known by *crus*, just like wines and champagnes. Cheese features large on any menu and restaurants in Normandy tend to keep up the proper tradition of the cheese course. Three of the best known are Camembert, Pont l'Eveque and Livarot. Cattle in this major dairy area are more often served as veal. *Pré-salé* lamb is a particular speciality of the western Manche coast, reared on the salt marshes of the Mont Saint-Michel Bay area as well as on the salt meadows of the coastal havres and providing tender meat with distinct taste.

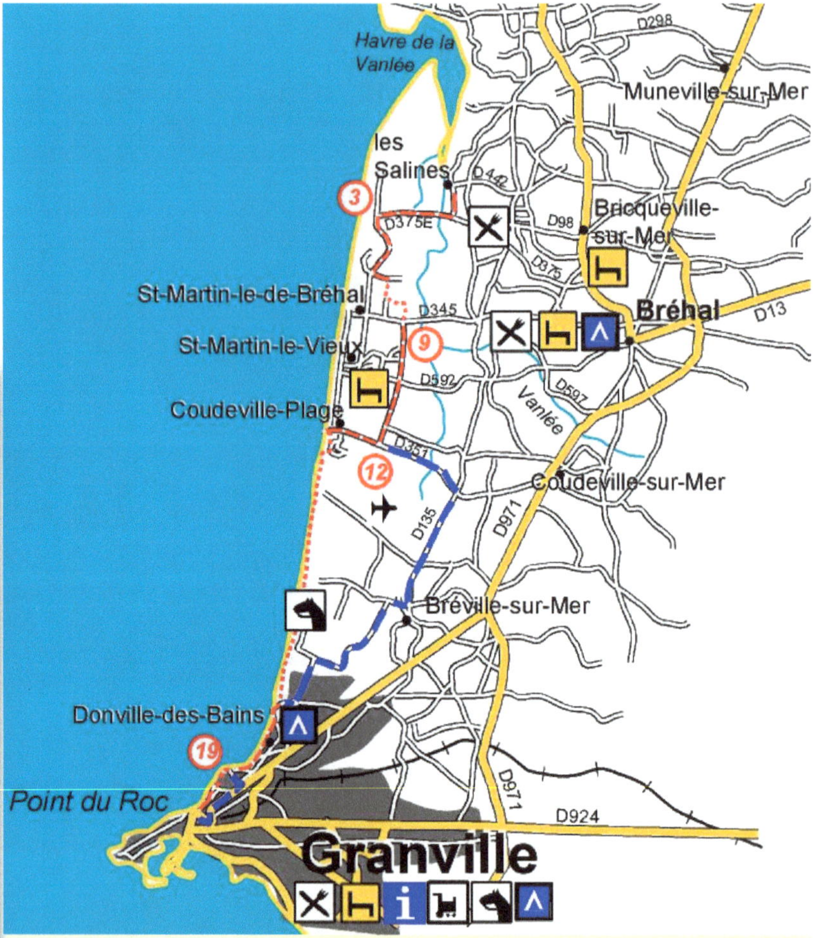

les Salines to Granville 12.8km

Route Summary: the route continues along the coast taking minor roads and tracks before joining the beach at Coudeville-sur-Mer. The beach is impossible for cyclists and restrictions apply for horse riders leading to a detour around the Granville airfield. The final entry to Granville follows a cliff top path where again steps require a diversion onto the main road for horse and bike riders.

Way Point	Distance	Directions	Verification Point	Compass
1		From the junction in les Salines continue south with the estuary immediately to the right	Havre de la Vanlée	S
2	500	Turn right to cross the estuary. **Note:** the area ahead is liable to flooding. In this event, turn left and after 300 metres turn right. In a further 1.5 kilometres turn right onto the D345 and cross the waterway by the bridge	Beside the restaurant la Paserelle	W
3	1300	After crossing Havre de la Vanlée, turn left at the road junction. Avoid the pathway signs crossing the grass		S
4	600	Remain on the road and pass beside a campsite -		SW
5	400	Turn left	Opposite the entrance to la Vanlée campsite	E
6	300	At a crossroads in tracks, turn right		S
7	300	At the next crossroads turn left		E
8	200	Follow the track as it bears right in the direction of the bridge		S
9	300	At the crossroads beside the bridge go straight ahead on the rue des Goélettes	Between the waterway and the Hippodrome	S
10	800	At the crossroads with the D592, go straight across	Rue des Disquiets	S
11	300	Continue straight along the road	Pass beside a stable	S
12	600	At the T-junction take a right on the D351 in the direction of Coudeville-Plage. **Note:-** the route ahead takes you onto the beach. Loose sand makes cycling impossible, while there are also restrictions for horses on the beach. Riders are advised to turn left on the D351 and then at the crossroads turn right on the D135 to Bréville-sur-Mer. In Bréville turn right on avenue de la Plage and the first left passing beside the Hippodrome. At the T-junction turn right and then left on rue du Champ de Courses. At the T-junction with the rue de l'Hermitage turn right and rejoin the main route at Way Point #16	Airfield ahead	W
13	700	Facing the sea with Coudeville-sur-Mer behind you take the left onto a stone track		S

les Salines to Granville 12.8km

Way Point	Distance	Directions	Verification Point	Compass
14	300	Bear right and follow the beach towards Granville	Pass airfield to the left	S
15	4000	Turn left to leave the beach and enter a car park between a tall modern building with brown verandas and the Relais Voile		S
16	160	Pass on the landward side of the large building and turn right onto rue de la Plage. **Note**:- cyclists and riders rejoin from the left	Wooded cliffs to the left	SW
17	800	As you climb the hill and the road turns inland, take a right turn onto a pathway above the cliffs	White railings	SW
18	70	At the top of the hill, turn right with the sea on your right.	Rue de la Douane	W
19	400	At the junction of the rue de la Douane and the rue du 8 mai 1945, take the small path to the right. **Note**:- there is a flight of steps ahead and so horse and bike riders should turn left on the rue du 8 mai 1945 and then right at the main road, route de Coutances to the end of this section beside Hôtel des Bains	Continuing above cliffs	SW
20	300	Go straight ahead on the Chemin de Noroit		SW
21	200	At crossroads turn right	Rue de la Falaise	SW
22	200	Pass Hôtel le Grand Large and at the junction beside Hôtel Michelet take the steeply descending road to the right.		SW
23	150	Descend on the rue Jules Michlelet and enter rue des Juifs beside the Hôtel des Bains		

les Salines to Granville 12.8km

Accommodation	Price	Opening	Animals
Le Salin, Rond-Point des Français Libres 50290 BRÉHAL Tel: 0033 (0)2 33 50 28 80	B2	All Year	🐴
Hôtel Restaurant la Gare, 1 pl Comdt Godard 50290 BREHAL Tel: 0033 (0)2 33 61 61 11	B3	All Year	🐴
Bloquet Evelyne, 11 Le Mesnil 50290 BRÉHAL Tel: 0033 (0)2 33 61 38 33 bigbeni@club.fr	B2	All Year	🚫
Bois André, 8 chem Moignerie 50290 BRICQUEVILLE SUR MER Tel: 0033 (0)2 33 61 63 22	B2	All Year	🐴
Guindre Alain, Bord 87700 SAINT MARTIN LE VIEUX Tel: 0033 (0)5 55 39 19 84	B2	All Year	🐴
Hôtel Restaurant Le Relais des Iles, 3 av Mer 50290 COUDEVILLE SUR MER Tel: 0033 (0)2 33 61 66 66	B2	All Year	🐴
Hôtel Michelet, 5 r Jules Michelet 50400 GRANVILLE Tel: 0033 (0)2 33 50 06 55	B2	All Year	🐴
Benoist Albert, 2 Le Tilleul 50400 GRANVILLE Tel: 0033 (0)2 33 90 76 11 benoistrene@tele2.fr	B2	20/03-31/12	🐴
Mauduit D, 93 imp Pavillons 50400 GRANVILLE Tel: 0033 (0)2 33 50 43 56	B2	All Year	🐴
Camping	**Price**	**Opening**	**Animals**
Camping de la Vanlée, La Vanlée 50290 BRÉHAL Tel: 0033 (0)2 33 61 63 80	B1	01/05-01/09	🐴
La Route Blanche, 6 La Route Blanche 50290 BRÉVILLE SUR MER Tel: 0033 (0)2 33 50 23 31 larouteblanche@camping-breville.com campinglarouteblanche.com	B1	01/04- 31/10	🐴
Camping de l'Ermitage Intercommunal, r Ermitage 50350 DONVILLE LES BAINS Tel: 0033 (0)2 33 50 09 01 camping-ermitage@wanadoo.fr	B1	All Year	🐴
L' Oasis de la Plage, rte Champ de Courses 50350 DONVILLE LES BAINS Tel: 0033 (0)2 33 50 52 01	B1	All Year	🐴
Camping La Vague, 126 rte Vaudroulin 50400 GRANVILLE Tel: 0033 (0)2 33 50 29 97	B1	15/04-01/09	🐴
Youth Hostel	**Price**	**Opening**	**Animals**
Centre Regional de Nautisme, Bd des Amiraux 50400 Granville Tel: 0033 (0)2 33 91 22 62 crng50@wanadoo.fr	B1	All Year	🚫
Equestrian Centre			
Club Hippique de Granville, 1 imp Dunes 50290 BREVILLE SUR MER Tel: 0033 (0)2 33 50 22 16			
Chemin Philippe, Prétot 50400 GRANVILLE Tel: 0033 (0)2 33 50 09 30			

les Salines to Granville 12.8km

Useful Contacts
Tourist Offices
Office de Tourisme, 4 crs Jonville 50400 GRANVILLE   Tel:0033 (0)2 33 91 30 03
Doctor
Rouleau Olivier, 10 r Port de Jaf 50400 GRANVILLE   Tel: 0033 (0)2 33 50 06 61
Veterinary
 Lamy François, 2 r Doct Benoît 50400 GRANVILLE   Tel: 00 33 (0)2 33 50 33 78
Farriers
Pitrey Didier, 11 r Croix Layné 50320 BEAUCHAMPS Tel: 0033 (0)2 33 51 63 68
Note: 18km from Granville

les Salines to Granville 12.8km

Granville has a history of piracy as seen in the severe citadel of Haute Ville guarding the approaches to the bay of Mont St-Michel. The old town preserves all the history of its military and religious past. The lower town was partly built on land reclaimed from the sea. The upper part of the old town is surrounded by ramparts from the 15th century. These are entered through the drawbridge,   Grand'Porte. Inside the walls of the upper town are some beautiful houses of which several are concentrated on Rue Saint-Jean. The ancient church of Notre-Dame du Cap Lihou built during the Hundred Years' War out of granite, dominates the heights and constitutes an imposing building of the Romanesque style. There is a museum located in one of the gates which preserves invaluable documents relating to the history of the town through the centuries. Granville also is the home of the Musée Christian Dior, located in the fashion designer's childhood home, Villa Les Rhumbs.
Also of interest: Isles of Chausey. Sailings from beginning of April until end of September. Daily crossings every 50 min.
Tel : 0033 (0) 825 138 050 info@compagniecorsaire.com

Routy Summary: the route initially climbs into the high old town of Granville and then proceeds along the coast. The walker's path takes to the cliff tops with ascents and descents to the beaches. Horse riders and cyclists are advised to avoid the steepest sections. From Karion Plage the route swings inland through farm land on pleasant tracks but again riders are provided with an alternate route to avoid the most difficult sections.

Way Point	Distance	Directions	Verification Point	Compass
1		From Hôtel des Bains proceed along rue des Juifs		SW
2	70	Walkers turn right and take the flight of steps from Place du Maréchal Foch to the Cité Historique and the Musée d'Art. **Note**:- horse and bike riders can enter the Cité Historique by remaining on the Rue des Juifs and taking the first turning to the right and then right again on the rue Notre Dame to rejoin the main route in Place de l'Isthme at Way Point #4	Casino to the right	NW
3	60	At the top of the steps bear right		NW
4	90	Continue around the ramparts with the sea on the right	Place de l'Isthme	W
5	300	Emerge from under an arch and continue straight ahead along the Promenade Charles VII into a "no entry" road	Rue du Nord	SW
6	200	At the T-junction turn right and follow the rue du Roc		SW
7	80	Pass through the gates and enter an area surrounded by grand municipal buildings. **Note**:- cyclists and horse riders should avoid the cliff path and bear left leaving the old town via the Boulevard des Terre-Neuviers and rejoin the main route at Way Point #11 overlooking the port.		W
8	100	After going through the gates turn right into the car park and head for sandy path	Cliffs immediately to the right	W
9	500	After crossing the grass towards the lighthouse keep to the path along the top of the cliffs	Below a gun turret	S
10	250	Follow the Promenade du Roc around the Cap		E
11	300	The path emerges on the rue du Port, continue straight ahead. **Note**:- Riders rejoin from the left	Signed *Centre Ville*	NE
12	600	At the roundabout turn right	Direction Avranches	E
13	150	Follow the dockside on Boulevard des Amiraux Granvillais		SE

Granville to Carolles Plage 15.9km

Way Point	Distance	Directions	Verification Point	Compass
14	200	At the Zone Portuaire the path turns right to leave the road	Pass alongside the Centre Régional de Nautisme	SE
15	90	Turn left behind the Centre Régional de Nautisme , continue straight ahead beside the sea	Through a white metal gate and into the boatyard	E
16	190	Return to the road and turn right		SE
17	160	Follow the busy Boulevard des Amiraux Granvillais and rue Saint Gaud	Up the hill	E
18	200	Walkers turn right up a flight of wooden steps into a small parking area. **Note:-** the next section includes narrow cliff paths and flights of steps. Cyclists and horse riders are advised to remain on the D911 travelling parallel to the sea-shore to Way Point #26 where the road runs close to the cliff tops after passing the headland of la Crête		SE
19	50	At the top of the steps turn left		E
20	100	Just before the end of the road take the Sentier Littoral to the right - a narrow gravel track		SE
21	500	After a flight of steps, turn right on the road	Cale d'Haqueville	SW
22	50	At fork bear left on Impasse du Port Foulon	White house on the left	S
23	90	Bear left up hill on a grassy track	Sign Voie Privé	S
24	200	Take the right fork onto the lower track towards sea.		S
25	100	Climb flight of stone steps and proceed on cliff top path		SE
26	500	The track brings you back onto the main road, turn right with sea on your right	D911	SE
27	600	At the intersection with the D572 continue on the D911 towards Saint-Pair-sur-Mer	Pass through St Nicolas Plage	S
28	600	At the entry to Saint-Pair-sur-Mer take the right fork away from the major road	Pass to the right of the church	S
29	70	Take the first turning to the right	Rue St Pierre	W
30	70	Turn left at the sea and follow the narrow tarmac track		S
31	300	Turn left into the town	Rue de Scissy	E

Granville to Carolles Plage 15.9km

Way Point	Distance	Directions	Verification Point	Compass
32	190	Turn right at the T-junction and rejoin the main road	Rue Charles Mathuin, D911	S
33	500	Just before reaching brow of hill, turn right, between houses, and take a gravelled cycle track	Sign Kairon Plage	SE
34	400	Straight ahead through car park beside the beach	Kairon Plage	S
35	300	Exit the car park and turn left across the road. Take the minor road D569	Route de Catteville	E
36	50	Immediately turn right on road which quickly changes to a gravelled track	Chemin de Beau Soleil	SE
37	900	The track brings you out onto a tarmac road, turn right	GR223	S
38	120	On the crown of the bend, bear left on the track	Chemin du Verchu	SE
39	200	Take the right fork		S
40	500	At the next fork bear left		SE
41	500	At the crossroads, turn right	Village of Kairon	S
42	110	Just in front of church turn left. **Note:**- the route ahead has a difficult river crossing and narrow pathways. Cyclists and horse riders should continue on the D154 and bear left along the rue du Pont Hogris into Jullouville. Take the next left turn on the avenue de Kairon and continue along the Chemins des Cols Verts. Turn right on Route de Bouillon and follow the road to the foot of the steps descending the steep hillside in Carolles Plage - Way Point #61		SE
43	60	Go straight on through the farm yard		E
44	400	At a T-junction with a small tarmac road, turn right		S
45	140	The road ends in a grassy track, turn left down a very narrow path		E
46	90	Turn right		SE
47	300	Keep to the path along the edge of the fields		S
48	250	Cross over the river Thar	Narrow footbridge	E
49	200	At the T-junction with a broader track, turn right		E
50	300	At the crossroads with a tarmac road, turn right.		S

Granville to Carolles Plage 15.9km

Way Point	Distance	Directions	Verification Point	Compass
51	300	At the T-junction with the D109 turn right	Towards the centre of Bouillon	SW
52	70	Turn left	Chemin des Carrouges	S
53	400	Turn right	Chemin de Chevrue	SW
54	300	At the crossroads go straight ahead on the D471 in the direction of Bouillon		SW
55	400	At the crossroads with the D571 go straight over	Chemin des Montes	W
56	600	Take the right fork.		SW
57	900	At the T-junction turn right		W
58	200	Turn left	Beside the woods	SW
59	80	Continue on the dirt track straight ahead		SW
60	200	Turn right down a long flight of steps		W
61	90	At the foot of the escarpment turn left		SW
62	100	Arrive in Carolles Plage at the junction with the D911	Rue Vauban	

Granville to Carolles Plage 15.9km

Useful Contacts

Tourist Offices

Office de Tourisme, 33bis, rue de la Poste 50740 Carolles
Tel: 00 33 (0)2 .33 61 92 88   carolles.tourisme(at)wanadoo.fr

Saint-Pair-sur-Mer Office de Tourisme 50380 SAINT-PAIR-SUR-MER
Tel: 0033 (0)2 33 50 52 77   offitour.st.pair.s.mer@wanadoo.fr
www.saintpairsurmer.com

Internet Cafes

Archesys, 16 r de L'Union 50100 CHERBOURG Tel: 0033 0(2) 33 53 04 93

Doctor

Chevalier Marie-Laure, 3 r Placin 50740 CAROLLES Tel: 0033 (0)2 33 91 22 75

Farrier

Guernigou François, 4 La Croix Virette 50530 GENETS Tel: 0033 (0)2 33 48 49 98

Accommodation	Price	Opening	Animals
Hotel les Pins, 38 avenue de la Libération 50610 JULLOUVILLE Tel: 0033 (0)2 33 61 81 63	B1	All Year	🐎
Hotel des Falaises, 45 Avenue Vauban 50610 JULLOUVILLE Tel: 0033 (0)2 33 61 83 29	B2	All Year	🐎
Mme CARUHEL, 3379 la Maréchallerie 50380 SAINT PAIR SUR MER Tel: 0033 (0)2 33 51 65 37 Mobile: 0033 (0)6 61 11 65 37 caruhelclaudine@orange	B2	All Year	🐎
Levavasseur, 34 bis rue de la Croix 50740 CAROLLES Tel: 0033 (0)2 33 51 62 69	B2	All Year	🐎
LEFEUVRE Solange et Louis, 3 impasse du Puits 50740 CAROLLES Tel: 0033 (0)2 33 58 05 40 Mobile: 0033 (0)6 84 77 21 18	B2	All Year	🐎

Camping	Price	Opening	Animals
Camping Lez Eaux, 451 rte Guigeois 50380 SAINT PAIR SUR MER Tel: 0033 (0)2 33 51 66 09 www.lez-eaux.com/tarifs_camping.php	B1	29/03-30/10	🐎
Camping de l'Ecutot, rte Ecutot 50380 SAINT PAIR SUR MER Tel: 0033 (0)2 33 50 26 29	B1	01/06-15/11	🐎
Etoile de Mer 50380 KAIRON PLAGE Tel: 0033 (0)2 33 50 78 07 camping.etoiledemer@wanadoo.fr	B1	01/06-03/09	🐎
Camping La Guérinière, Rue des Jaunets 50740 CAROLLES Tel: 0033 (0)2 33 61 93 75	B1	01/04-30/10	🐎

Equestrian Centre

Centre Equestre de Kairon Plage, Chemin du Petit Kairon 50380 SAINT-PAIR-SUR-MER Tel: 0033 (0)2 33 51 21 80

Cottin Patrice, chem Petit Kairon 50380 SAINT PAIR SUR MER Tel: 0033 (0)2 33 51 21 80

Granville to Carolles Plage 15.9km

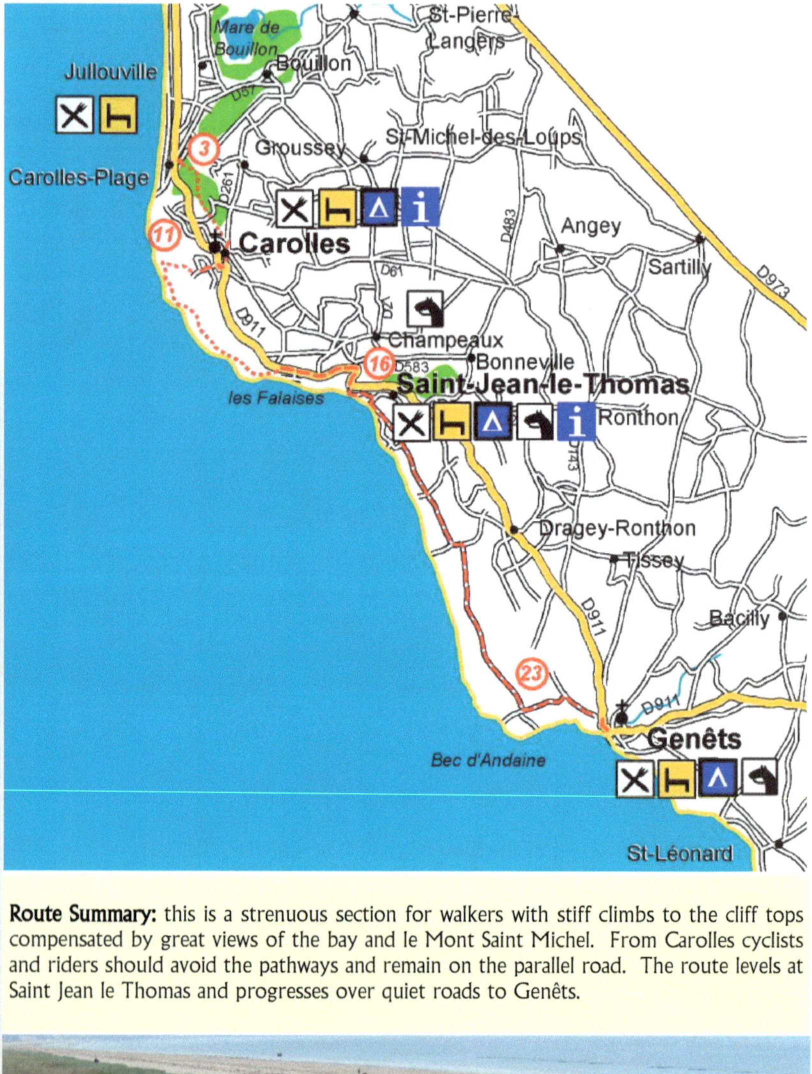

Carolles-Plage to Genêts 15.2km

Route Summary: this is a strenuous section for walkers with stiff climbs to the cliff tops compensated by great views of the bay and le Mont Saint Michel. From Carolles cyclists and riders should avoid the pathways and remain on the parallel road. The route levels at Saint Jean le Thomas and progresses over quiet roads to Genêts.

Way Point	Distance	Directions	Verification Point	Compass
1		From the junction between the D911 and Avenue de la Poste take Avenue de la Poste and turn sharp right to return to the foot of the long flight of steps descending the wooded escarpment		NE
2	300	Turn right keeping the steps and the escarpment to your left and take the pathway that skirts the escarpment and enter the woods	GR223	SE
3	600	Take the bridge over the gorge and keep straight on the disused railway track until reaching the village of Carolles		SE
4	1000	At the cross-roads with route de Groussey, cross straight over		SE
5	80	Turn right towards the church		SW
6	90	Turn left and leave Carolles on rue de la Poste		S
7	180	At the fork in the road, turn right. **Note:-** the cliff path ahead is extremely narrow with many steep sections. Cyclists and riders should go straight ahead in the direction of St Jean le Thomas on the D911. The main route will rejoin the D911 at Way Point #15 near the parking area in les Falaises		W
8	110	Turn left on the crown of the bend	GR223	SW
9	300	Take the road to the right		N
10	30	Turn left on an unmade track		W
11	700	Turn left over a small concrete bridge	Sign for the Sentier Littoral in the direction la Cabane Vauban.	SW
12	90	At the top of the steep climb take the path to the left	Keep sea to the right	SE
13	900	At an intersection of tracks continue straight on	Sentier Littoral sign for St Jean le Thomas	SE
14	1900	Pass between 2 buildings and turn left towards the main road		E
15	90	Turn right on the D911		E
16	1200	After 2 successive sharp bends to the right, take the turning to the right on a narrow road and descend the hill		SE

Carolles-Plage to Genêts 15.2km

Way Point	Distance	Directions	Verification Point	Compass
17	400	At the T-junction turn right, towards the sea, on the D241	Rue Gustav Belloir, St Jan le Thomas to the left	W
18	80	Turn left onto the Boulevard Stanislas. The road runs parallel to the beach		SE
19	800	At the crossroads go straight on	Chemin Montois	SE
20	1000	At the next crossroads again go straight ahead		SE
21	900	At the T-junction turn left	Right angles to the sea	E
22	80	Turn right and continue parallel to the sea shore		S
23	2800	At the T-junction with the D35el turn left. **Note:-** the departure point for the bay crossing le Bec d'Andaine is to the right		E
24	700	At the next T junction turn right remaining on the D35el		SE
25	700	At the T-junction with the D911 turn right and enter Genêts		SE
26	200	Arrive in the centre of Genêts beside the church on rue de l'Entreponts		

Carolles-Plage to Genêts 15.2km

St Jean-le-Thomas church dates from the mid 11th century, despite a number of re-workings in the 12th century. The walls retain fragments of wall paintings, which probably covered the entire interior of the building. Two distinct sets can be discerned. The one, located on the tympanum of a portal walled up in the mid-12th century, dates from the end of the 11th and is the oldest example of Romanesque painting in Normandy. The scene represents shows a conflict involving Jacob fighting the Angel. The second set from the second half of the 12th century covers part of the south wall of the nave. The scenes - the story of Cain and Abel - take place on two superimposed registers, separated by bands and tracery patterns.

Accommodation	Price	Opening	Animals
Collard Gérald, 11 r Mar Leclerc 50530 SAINT JEAN LE THOMAS Tel: 0033 (0)2 33 48 84 19 geraldcollard@equitation-collard.com	B2	All Year	🐴
Leroy André et Suzanne, 7 av Libération 50530 SAINT JEAN LE THOMAS Tel: 0033 (0)2 33 60 10 02	B2	All Year	🐴
Hôtel Restaurant des Bains, 8 allée Clémenceau 50530 SAINT JEAN LE THOMAS Tel: 0033 (0)2 33 48 84 20 hdbains@orange.fr http://hotel-sejour-restaurant-logis-de-france-granville-avranches.hdesbains.fr/	B3	All Year	🐴
Daniel Louis, 93 Grande Rue 50530 GENETS Tel: 0033 (0)2 33 70 83 78	B2	All Year	🐴
Camping	Price	Opening	Animals
Gaslain Yvette, 1 La Péramé 50530 GENETS Tel: 0033 (0)2 33 70 82 49	B1	All Year	🐴
Camping Les Coques d'Or, 14 rte Bec d'Andaine 50530 GENETS Tel: 0033 (0)2 33 70 82 57	B1	All Year	🐴
Plage Pignochet 50530 SAINT JEAN LE THOMAS Tel: 0033 (0)2 33 48 84 02	B1	01/03-15/11	🐴
Youth Hostel	Price	Opening	Animals
28 Rue de l'Ortillon 50530 GENÊTS Tel: 0033 (0)2 33 58 40 16 genets@fuaj.org	B1	All Year	❌

Equestrian Centre,

Ferme Equestre des Courlisn, 2 rte De la parisière 50530 CHAMPEAUX Tel: 0033 (0)2 33 51 89 23

Letreguilly Jean-paul, 14 chem MONTOIS 50530 SAINT JEAN LE THOMAS Tel: 0033 (0)2 33 89 58 32

Collard Gérald, 11 r Mar Leclerc 50530 SAINT JEAN LE THOMAS Tel: 0033 (0)2 33 48 84 19

Centre Equestre Du Bec D'Andaine, 50530 GENETS Mobile: 0033 (0)6 80 48 31 62

Everwyn Marc, 1 Le Fresnay 50530 GENETS Tel: 0033 (0)2 33 60 38 88 Mobile: 0033 (0)9 79 25 96 78

Useful Contacts
Tourist Offices
Syndicat D'initiative, 13 r Pierre le Jaudet 50530 SAINT JEAN LE THOMAS Tel: 0033 (0)2 33 70 90 71 stjlethomas@wanadoo.fr www.stjeanlethomas.com
Doctor
Longvilliers Charles, 32 pl Halles 50530 GENETS Tel: 0033 (0)2 33 70 87 87
Farrier
Guernigou François, 4 La Croix Virette 50530 GENETS Tel: 0033 (0)2 33 48 49 98

Carolles-Plage to Genêts 15.2km

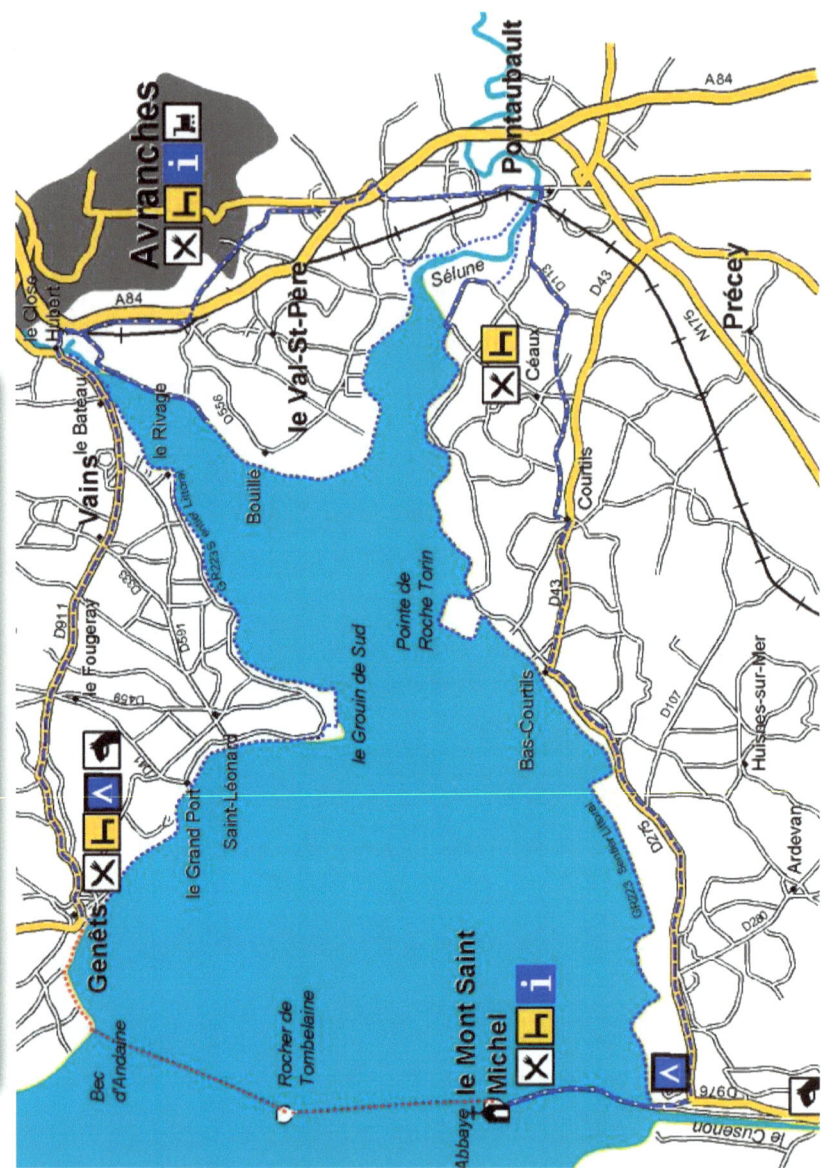

This section offers three options according to your own preferences and mode of transport:
1. Bay crossing (with guide) on foot — 7.2km
2. Round the bay on foot, generally small tracks and beachside paths, with a small section of road for the river crossing — 39.2km
3. Round the bay for bicycles — 29.1km

Accommodation - many options available, selection below	Price	Opening	Animals
Hôtel Patton Citotel, 93 r Constitution 50300 AVRANCHES Tel: 0033 (0)2 33 48 52 52	B2	All Year	
La Renaissance, 15 r Fosses 50300 AVRANCHES Tel: 0033 (0)2 33 58 03 71	B2	All Year	
Bar Hotel Brasserie du Jardin des Plantes, 10 pl Carnot 50300 AVRANCHES Tel: 0033 (0)2 33 58 03 68	B2	All Year	
Hôtel de La Croix d'Or, 83 r Constitution 50300 AVRANCHES Tel: 0033 (0)2 33 58 04 88	B2	All Year	
Brit Hotel Le Relais Du Mont, La Buvette, Ceaux Le Mont Saint Michel 50220 Tel: 0033 (0)2 33 70 92 55 e.relais.du.mont@wanadoo.fr	B2	All Year	
Hotels inside the walls of Mont St Michel			
Le Saint-Michel Ridel, Rue Principale 50170 LE MONT SAINT-MICHEL Tel: 0033 (0)2 33 60 14 37	B3	All Year	
Hôtel Duguesclin, Grande Rue 50170 MONT SAINT MICHEL Tel: 0033 (0)2 33 60 14 10	B3	All Year	
Camping	**Price**	**Opening**	**Animals**
Camping Caravaning Du Mont Saint Michel, rte Mont 50170 MONT SAINT MICHEL Tel: 0033 (0)2 33 60 22 10	B1	All Year	
Equestrian Centre,			
Centre Equestre La Tanière, Baie du Mont Saint Michel 50170 MOIDRE Tel: 0033 (0)2 33 58 13 53			

Useful Contacts

Tourist Offices

Office du Tourisme, Corps de Garde des Bourgeois bd Avancée 50170 MONT SAINT MICHEL Tel: 0033 (0)2 33 60 14 30
Office du Tourisme, bd Avancée 50170 MONT SAINT MICHEL
Tel: 0033 (0)2 33 60 14 30

Doctor

David Martine, 20 pl Littré 50300 AVRANCHES Tel: 0033 (0)2 33 58 67 15

Farrier

Clinique Vétérinaire des Docteurs Coulon Jean-François et Gosselin Christophe, 12 r St Saturnin 50300 AVRANCHES   Tel: 0033 (0)2 33 58 61 55

When you finally reach the mythical monument, the silhouette of which has been visible for miles, it is easy to imagine how impatient pilgrims must have felt back in the days when a long and difficult journey finally brought them to the foot of Mont Saint Michel. Rising from a hazy expanse of sand and waves, Mont Saint Michel appears like man's defiance of the elements and of time. A rock lost in a landscape smoothed by the wind. Suspended high on the rock, the abbey is a testament to the wild ambition of its builders. Legend has it that in 708, Aubert, Bishop of the nearby town of Avranches, was visited by Saint Michael in a dream and ordered to turn the Mont into a shrine to him. Aubert, thinking he had imagined it, did nothing. The archangel grew impatient and, when he appeared for the third time, poked a hole in the disbeliever's skull. He also performed many miracles to convince the Bishop and Christians. A stolen bull was found at the top of the Mont, as Saint Michael had predicted, and according to one story, Aubert's oratory was built on the area of land trampled by it. According to another, the oratory was built on the area left dry by morning dew. Aubert finally fulfilled the archangel's wishes and sent messengers to Monte Gargano in Italy to report the events. As a result sacred relics were sent back, including a piece of red cloak worn by the archangel during one of his apparitions and a fragment of the altar where he had placed his foot. Divine intervention is said to have subsequently facilitated the men's work. An old man from the locality, called by God, managed to move a large rock, though another version claims a child touched the rock with his foot and sent it tumbling into the abyss. Similarly, although there was no drinking water on the mount, a spring, the fountain of St Aubert, was miraculously discovered. The consecration of the Mont (for which there is no historic documentation apart from a much later account, the Revelation), gave rise to marvellous legends that enchanted Christians and on which the first historians later relied. Over time the rock became known as Mont-Saint-Michel and Aubert sent monks to live there and pray to God and his archangel.

From the middle of the 13th century to the beginning of the 16th century, monks completed the ring around the church on the east and south by constructing the abbot's residence and buildings to house the abbey's legal and administrative services. During the Hundred Years' War, the village at the foot of the abbey was surrounded by massive ramparts. The heroic resistance of Mont Saint-Michel against the English making the abbey a national symbol. The choir of the church, which collapsed in 1421, was replaced in peacetime by a flamboyant Gothic structure. In 1790, the monks left their monastery, which was used as a prison until 1863. After this it was designated a historical monument, major works were undertaken to restore the monument to its former splendour and today it is a focal point for pilgrims, historians and tourists alike.

Pilgrims on their way to the Mont were known as *miquelots.*, and like other pilgrims, they could be recognised by their *besace*, a leather pouch carried over the right shoulder and their bourdon, a roughly hewn staff. In addition to the traditional, multilingual pilgrim medley, children and teenagers started to make their way to the Mont from the early 14th century onwards and up until the French Revolution. Sometimes no more than eight years old, these young pilgrims became known as the *pastoureaux* (shepherds) and came from as far afield as the Rhineland and the south of France.

After the festivities celebrating the abbey's one thousandth anniversary in 1966, it was taken over by a Benedictine order. In 2001, the Bishop of Coutances and Avranches asked the Freres et Soeurs Monastiques de Jerusalem to assume this spiritual role. The monks and nuns live near their primary church, Saint-Gervais-Saint-Protais, work part-time in the town and follow the rules of a *Book of Life*. The Community celebrates Sunday Mass at 11.30 and Tuesday-Saturday daily at 12.15.

Genêts, formerly a very active town and port, depended a great deal on the revenue derived from the pilgrims crossing the bay to Mont St Michel.

Mont Saint Michel is situated in a bay of 40,000 hectares, traversed by three rivers, the Couesnon, the Sée and the Sélune, and washed twice a day by tides described by Victor Hugo as *"à la vitesse d'un cheval au galop"* or "as swiftly as a galloping horse". The tide actually comes in at one metre per second.

To go to and from the island, pilgrims either took a boat or, more often, they waited for the low tide in order to walk across the freshly exposed sands. Many miscalculated the tidal cycles and drowned, while some were swallowed by the perilous quicksand. A causeway was built in 1879 and now contributes to the silting up of the bay, damming the incoming water and robbing Mont St Michel of its true island status. In June 2006, the French prime minister announced a €164 million project (Projet Mont-Saint-Michel) to build a hydraulic dam that will help remove the accumulated silt and make Mont Saint-Michel an island again. It is expected to be completed by 2012.

At full moon the sea covers the more than 15 kilometres from its low point at the coast right up to Mont Saint Michel. Undoubtedly a magnificent natural spectacle, but also dangerous. Visitors are strongly advised to cross only with a professional guide (details below) or alternatively take a bus round the bay.

Contact Information for Guided Walks Across Mont St Michel Bay

Groupement d'Intérêt Touristique du Pays de la Baie du Mont-Saint-Michel, 5 bis place de la Cathédrale 35120 Dol-de-Bretagne Tel: 0033 (0)2 99 48 34 53
info@paysdelabaie-mtstmichel.com

For online request form: www.paysdelabaie-mtstmichel.com/fr/contact/index.asp

Maison de la baie Relais de Genêts, Place de la Mairie 50530 Genêts
Tel: 0033 (0)2 33 89 64 00   maison.baie.genets@wanadoo.fr

Bus Timetable Genêts to Mont St Michel

Depart	Arrive	Duration	Changes	Instructions
10.00	15.37	5.37	2	Wait in front of Genêts church. Take Bus No. 166, direction Avranches Place Littré. 10.20 Disembark at Avranches Place Littré (AVRANCHES). Walk to the stop at Avranches Place Littré and take bus No. 5 direction Pontorson Gare SNCF. 12.45 Disembark at Pontorson Gare SNCF (PONTORSON). Walk to the stop Pontorson Gare SNCF and take Bus No. 6 direction Mont St Michel Le Mont. 15.37 Disembark at Mont St Michel Le Mont.
13.30	18.11	4.41	2	
18.01	19.23	1.22	2	

Section Name	Distance	Scale	Map Reference no.	Title
Winchester to Bishop's Waltham	18100	1:50,000	ISBN: 9780319228845	Ordnance Survey Landranger Map – sheet 185, Winchester & Basingstoke
Bishop's Waltham to Portsmouth	27670	1:50,000	ISBN: 9780319228692	Ordnance Survey Landranger Map – sheet 196, The Solent & Isle of Wight
Barfleur to Saint-Vaast-le-Hougue	13310	1:25,000	1310OT	IGN Top 25, CHERBOURG/POINTE DE BARFLEUR
Saint-Vaast-la-Hougue to le Bourg de Lestre	11900	1:25,000	1310OT	IGN Top 25, CHERBOURG/POINTE DE BARFLEUR
		1:25,000	1311E	IGN Top 25, SAINTE-MERE-EGLISE/SAINTE-MARIE-DU-MONT/UTAH BEACH
le Bourg de Lestre to Montebourg	10770	1:25,000	1311E	IGN Top 25, SAINTE-MERE-EGLISE/SAINTE-MARIE-DU-MONT/UTAH BEACH
		1:25,000	1211E	IGN Top 25, VALOGNES/SAINT-SAUVEUR-LE-VICOMTE
Montebourg to Sainte-Mère-Eglise	11400	1:25,000	1211E	IGN Top 25, VALOGNES/SAINT-SAUVEUR-LE-VICOMTE
		1:25,000	1311E	IGN Top 25, SAINTE-MERE-EGLISE/SAINTE-MARIE-DU-MONT/UTAH BEACH
Sainte-Mère-Eglise to Sainte-Marie-du-Mont	11160	1:25,000	1311E	IGN Top 25, SAINTE-MERE-EGLISE/SAINTE-MARIE-DU-MONT/UTAH BEACH

Section Name	Distance	Scale	Map Reference no.	Title
Carentan to Saintenay	11920	1:25,000	1312E	IGN Top 25, CARENTAN
		1:25,000	1312O	IGN Top 25, CARENTAN
		1:25,000	1312O	IGN Top 25, PERIERS
Saintenay to Périers	12690	1:25,000	1312O	IGN Top 25, PERIERS
Périers to Saint-Saveur-Landelin	9430	1:25,000	1312O	IGN Top 25, PERIERS
		1:25,000	1313O	IGN Top 25, SAINT-SAUVEUR-LENDELIN
Saint-Saveur-Landelin to Coutances	11730	1:25,000	1313O	IGN Top 25, SAINT-SAUVEUR-LENDELIN
Coutances to Regnéville-sur-Mer	13900	1:25,000	1214ET	IGN Top 25, GRANVILLE/COUTANCES/ÎLES CHAUSEY
Regnéville-sur-Mer to les Salines	14400	1:25,000	1214ET	IGN Top 25, GRANVILLE/COUTANCES/ÎLES CHAUSEY
les Salines to Granville	12880	1:25,000	1214ET	IGN Top 25, GRANVILLE/COUTANCES/ÎLES CHAUSEY
Granville to Carolles-Plage	15920	1:25,000	1215ET	IGN Top 25, AVRANCHES/GRANVILLE/LE MONT-SAINT-MICHEL
Carolles-Plage to Genêts	15230	1:25,000	1215ET	IGN Top 25, AVRANCHES/GRANVILLE/LE MONT-SAINT-MICHEL
Genêts to le-Mont-Saint-Michel	8550	1:25,000	1215ET	IGN Top 25, AVRANCHES/GRANVILLE/LE MONT-SAINT-MICHEL

The longest journey begins with a single step
Lao Tzu

Name:	
Address:	
Date Started:	
Place Started:	
Date Ended:	
Signature:	
Horse:	
Bicycle:	
On Foot:	

Pilgrim record - Signature & Stamp

Pilgrim record - Signature & Stamp

Pilgrim record - Signature & Stamp

Pilgrim record - Signature & Stamp

Pilgrim record - Signature & Stamp	Pilgrim record - Signature & Stamp
Pilgrim record - Signature & Stamp	Pilgrim record - Signature & Stamp
Pilgrim record - Signature & Stamp	Pilgrim record - Signature & Stamp
Pilgrim record - Signature & Stamp	Pilgrim record - Signature & Stamp

Pilgrim record - Signature & Stamp	Pilgrim record - Signature & Stamp
Pilgrim record - Signature & Stamp	Pilgrim record - Signature & Stamp
Pilgrim record - Signature & Stamp	Pilgrim record - Signature & Stamp
Pilgrim record - Signature & Stamp	Pilgrim record - Signature & Stamp

www.ingramcontent.com/pod-product-compliance
Lightning Source LLC
Chambersburg PA
CBHW042312150426
43200CB00001B/2